Clear Confusion in English Words

CLEAR CONFUSION IN ENGLISH WORDS

Sadar Kaintura
(PGT English)
Jawahar Navodaya Vidyalaya
Gangarkot, Suyalbari,
Nainital, Uttarakhand

UNIVERSITY SCIENCE PRESS
(An Imprint of Laxmi Publications Pvt. Ltd.)
BANGALORE • CHENNAI • COCHIN • GUWAHATI • HYDERABAD
JALANDHAR • KOLKATA • LUCKNOW • MUMBAI • RANCHI
NEW DELHI • BOSTON, USA

Published by :
UNIVERSITY SCIENCE PRESS
(*An Imprint of Laxmi Publications Pvt. Ltd.*)
113, Golden House, Darya Ganj,
New Delhi-110 002

Phone : 011-43 53 25 00
Fax : 011-43 53 25 28

www.laxmipublications.com
info@laxmipublications.com

First Edition : 2014

OFFICES

✆ **Bangalore**	080-26 61 15 61	✆ **Chennai**	044-24 34 47 26
✆ **Cochin**	0484-237 70 04, 405 13 03	✆ **Guwahati**	0361-254 36 69, 251 38 81
✆ **Hyderabad**	040-24 65 23 33	✆ **Jalandhar**	0181-222 12 72
✆ **Kolkata**	033-22 27 43 84	✆ **Lucknow**	0522-220 95 78
✆ **Mumbai**	022-24 91 54 15, 24 92 78 69	✆ **Ranchi**	0651-220 44 64

UCC-9688-095-CLEAR CONF ENG-WORD-KAI C—

Typesetted at : Shubham Composer, New Delhi. Printed at : Repro Knowledgecast Limited, Thane

जी. एस. बोथ्याल
आयुक्त
G. S. Bothyal
Commissioner

नवोदय विद्यालय समिति
Navodaya Vidyalaya Samiti
मानव संसाधन विकास मंत्रालय
Ministry of Human Resource Development
(स्कूल शिक्षा और साक्षरता विभाग)
(Deptt. of school Education & Literacy)
भारत सरकार/Government of India

FROM THE COMMISSIONER'S DESK

This is a matter of immense pleasure that Mr Sadar Kaintura, PGT (English), Jawahar Navodaya Vidyalaya, Suyalbari, District Nainital, Uttarakhand has written a book "Clear Confusion in English Words", I do hope that this book will be useful for the learners of English language to clear inherent doubts in the usage of different identical words. This will certainly enable them to distinguish among the words having likeness in shape, sound or spellings. The students will acquire the competency to use the appropriate and correct words.

I extend my best wishes to the book and its author.

(G. S. Bothyal)

गिरीश चन्द्र
उपायुक्त (प्रभारी)

0522-2738692
0522-2768123(D)
Fax: 0522-2738695
Gram - NAVSAM
नवोदय विद्यालय समिति,
क्षेत्रीय कार्यालय
(An Autonomous Organization of Ministry of Human Resource Development, Govt. of India)

FROM THE DEPUTY COMMISSIONER'S DESK

I feel glad to write that Mr Sadar Kaintura, PGT English, JNV, Nainital (Uttarakhand) has written a book "Clear Confusion in English Words". He has made a unique collection of confusing and identical words with their meanings which will prove as a helping tool for the learners of English language to clear confusion and doubts in writing, speaking and understanding English. I appreciate this commendable effort of Mr Kaintura and I am confident that this book will be very much useful for all learners of English language.

I extend my blessings and best wishes for the success of this book.

(Girish Chandra)
Deputy Commissioner I/c

Jawahar Navodaya Vidyalaya
(Ministry of Human Resource Development)
Education Department (Govt. of India)
Gangarkot, Suyalbari,
Nainital – 263135 (U. K.)
email .jnv_nainital@ymail.com

जवाहर नवोदय विद्यालय
(मानव संसाधन विकास मंत्रालय)
शिक्षा विभाग (भारत सरकार)
गंगरकोट, सुयालबाड़ी,
नैनीताल - **263135** (उत्तराखंड)

Website www. jnvnainital.org

Phone No (फोन नं0) 9758218195

FOREWORD

There is no denying fact that the knowledge of English is becoming an inevitable necessity each day. In order to acquire a competency in this language the proper knowledge of words and their usage play a significant role. As there is a lot of confusion in English words, spelling, meanings and pronunciation the need arises to know the words intimately since there are several words identical in sound or shape and giving the different meanings.

Mr Sadar Kaintura has made a collection of such words with their meanings in form of a book "Clear Confusion in English Words". This book will prove very useful not only for the students of all standards but also for the general reader. It is hoped that this book will meet its destined objectives.

I extend my best wishes for the success of this book.

S. K. Tyagi
PRINCIPAL

Preface

Like any other languages English also has many words which are identical to other words in sound or spelling but convey different meanings. Besides homonyms and homophones there are some words which convey different meanings in different forms of parts of speech. Furthermore, there is a lot of confusion in the usage of many words. Such confusing words create difficulty in learning and understanding English. An effort has been made to collect such words along with their meanings indicating the parts of speech they belong. This will help the learners to know the accuracy in usage and understanding English easily.

Suggestions regarding the drawbacks latent and improvement required if any, will be warmly accepted and acknowledged.

Author

Contents

Abbreviations Used

abbre.	Abbreviation
adj.	Adjective
adv.	Adverb
auxi.	Auxiliary
conj.	Conjunction
det.	Determiner
esp.	Especially
excl.	Exclamation
interj.	Interjection
n.	Noun
object.	Objective case
opp.	Opposite
plu.	Plural
poss.	Possessive
p.p.	Past participle
pref.	Prefix
pron.	Pronoun
prep.	Preposition
p.t.	Past tense
singu.	Singular
sb.	Somebody
sth.	Something
suff.	Suffix
v.	Verb.

1

HOMONYMS

About	*adv.*	approximately.
	adv.	facing the opposite direction.
	prep.	connected with, next to sb/sth.
	prep.	surrounding sb/sth.
	adj.	to be close to sth.
Above	*prep.*	more than an amount or level.
	adv.	at or to a higher place.
	adv.	greater in number.
	adj.	mentioned previously.
Abstract	*adj.*	a quality, idea or feeling rather than a material object.
	n.	a type of painting.
	n.	a summary.
Act	*n.*	a particular thing done.
	n.	law or decision passed by a parliament.
	n.	one of the main division of a play.
	v.	to play a role in a play, film.
Address	*v.*	to speak to a group of people.
	n.	details of where sb lives or works.
Admit	*v.*	confess.
	v.	allow to enter.
Adopt	*v.*	to accept.
	v.	to take or claim as own.

Affair	*n.*	events of public interest.
	n.	a sexual relationship between two persons.
	n.	matters, business.
	n.	unusual object.
Affaire	*n.*	a love affair.
Afternoon	*n.*	the time after 12 mid day to 6 O'clock.
Afternoons	*adv.*	during afternoon every day.
Age	*n.*	how many years one has lived.
	v.	*aged, aged, aging.* process to become older,
	suff.	the action or result of sth, condition or state.
Ages	*n.*	a historical period, very long time.
Ahead	*adv.*	in advance, further, in front.
	adv.	before.
Alight	*v.*	to come out of a vehicle.
	adv & adj.	illumined.
Anchor	*n.*	a heavy metal object used to prevent the boat from moving away.
	n.	a person who anchors a programme on a stage etc.
Angle	*n.*	meeting of two lines.
	v.	to fish with a hook.
Ante	*pref.*	before in time or position.
	n.	player's stake in poker.
Apart	*adv.*	separated by a distance.
	adv.	not together.
Apostrophe	*n.*	a mark of punctuation. (')
	n.	a figures of speech.
Arch	*adj.*	chief, main.
	combining form.	chief, principal.
	n.	curved part of building.
Are	*strong form* of *be, plu* of *is.*	
	n.	a unit for measuring land area.
Ark	*n.*	a large boat, box.
	n.	a position from which sth is viewed.

Arm	*n.*	part of body.
	n.	sleeve.
	n.	wing.
	v.	to make weapons.
Art	*n.*	human skill.
	v.	used to mean 'are' usually in poetry.
Article	*n.*	any object, item.
	n.	a piece of writing.
	n.	a separate item in a legal agreement.
	n.	*det (a, an, the).*
As	*prep.*	to describe quality purpose etc.
	adv.	used to compare.
	conj.	because, although, regarding.
Ash	*n.*	a grey substance left after sth is burnt.
	n.	a tree with grey bark.
Ass	*n.*	a donkey.
	n.	fool.
Ate	*v.*	*p.t* of *eat.*
	suff.	full of or having quality of.
At home	*n.*	a party in sb's home.
	adj.	done or taking place at home.
August	*n.*	8th month of the year.
	adj.	solemn, majestic.
Auto	*n.*	a car.
	combining form.	of or by oneself.
Bachelor	*n.*	an unmarried man.
	n.	a person who obtains a degree after intermediate.
Back	*n.*	the hinder part of the body.
	adj.	located behind.
	v.	support.
Bag	*n.*	a small sack, container.
	v.	to put into bag, to win sth, claim sth.

Baggage	*n.*	luggage during travel.
	n.	the beliefs & attitudes obtained by past experiences.
Bail	*n.*	amount of money paid to the court for release until trial.
	v.	to throw water away from a boat.
Ball	*n.*	a round object, a ball to play with.
	n.	dance party.
Band	*n.*	a tie, a thin flat strip put around things.
	n.	a group of musicians.
Bank	*n.*	an organization which gives various financial services to the public.
	n.	side of river, canal etc.
	n.	mass of cloud, snow etc.
	n.	arrangement of parts of machines.
Bar	*n.*	a place to buy & drink alcohol.
	n.	a long straight piece of metal or wood.
	n.	a band of colours or light.
	n.	the profession of any kind of Lawyer.
	v.	to block path.
	v.	to prevent.
Becoming	*v.*	*become, became, become, becoming.*
	adj.	flattering.
	adj.	suitable or appropriate.
Bench	*n.*	a long seat.
The bench	*n.*	a judge in the court.
Bene	*n.*	prayer.
	pref.	well.
Berth	*n.*	a bed in a ship, train etc.
	n.	job.
Bid	*v.*	to command, to offer, to buy.
	v.	to bid goodbye.
	n.	an offer of price *esp.* at an auction.
Bile	*n.*	the liquid which the liver produces.
	n.	anger or hatred.

Bill	*n.*	invoice.
	n.	money *(note)*.
	n.	written suggestion for a new law presented in the parliament.
	n.	programme of entertainment at a theatre.
	n.	poster.
	n.	beak *(birds)*.
Bin	*n.*	a container to put waste in.
	v.	to throw sth away.
Binding	*adj.*	compulsory.
	n.	tying all pages in a book.
	v.	*bind, bound, bound, binding.* tie with rope, string etc.
Bit	*n.*	small piece, portion or quantity.
	n.	metal mouthpiece on a bridle.
	n.	cutting or drilling part of a tool.
	v.	*p.t.* of *bite.*
Bitch	*n.*	a female dog.
	v.	to make unkind & critical remarks about sb.
Blend	*v.*	mix or mingle.
	v.	look good together.
Blind	*adj.*	unable to see.
	n.	a covering for window.
	v.	to make blind.
Blinds	*n.*	*plu.* a screen of branches to protect men in trenches.
Block	*n.*	obstacle.
	v.	to stop sth to flow.
Blossom	*n.*	a flower.
	v.	to become healthy.
Blow	*n.*	hard stroke, sudden set back.
	v.	*blow, blew, blown.* to move *(wind)*.
	v.	to sound horn etc.
Bluster	*v.*	speak loudly or in a bullying way.
	n.	empty threats or protests.

Board	*n.*	a piece of wood etc.
	n.	group of people.
	n.	meals provided in a hotel etc.
	v.	get on plane, ship.
Boil	*v.*	cook by the process of boiling.
	n.	red pus filled swelling on the skin.
Book	*n.*	printed pages with binding to read or write.
	v.	to arrange the room or seat.
Bore	*v.*	make a hole with a drill.
	v.	make sb feel weary & bored.
	n.	high wave caused by tide.
	v.	*bear, bore, borne.*
	n.	an uninteresting person.
Bosom	*n.*	a woman's breasts.
	n.	a situation in which sb is loved & protected.
Bound	*adj.*	certain or likely to happen.
	adj.	forced to do sth by law, duty etc.
	v.	*p.t & p.p.* of *bind.* to tie sb/sth with rope.
	v.	*bound, bounded, bounded.* to run with long steps.
	n.	a high or long jump.
Bow	*n.*	by which we shoot arrows.
	v.	to bend as a sign of respect.
Bowel	*n.*	the entrails.
	v.	to pass solid waste out of the body.
Bowl	*n.*	round container with an open top.
	n.	large heavy ball.
	v.	to roll ball, to play with bowls.
Boy	*n.*	a male child.
	excl.	we say when we express surprise or pain etc.
Brake	*n.*	a place over grown with wild plants, hedges etc.
	n.	a block to stop.
Break	*v.*	*broke, broken.* to shatter.
	n.	an interruption.
	v.	to show an opening.

Breed	*v.*	to beget.
	v.	a certain class of animals.
Brood	*v.*	to think deeply for long time.
	n.	offspring *(birds)* born at the same time.
	n.	a large family of children.
Buffet	*v.*	to push roughly.
	n.	a meal at which people serve themselves from a table.
Buoy	*n.*	an object floating on the sea to warn ships.
	v.	to make sb feel confident.
Burst	*n.*	a short period of a particular activity.
	v.	break into pieces.
But	*conj.*	however, yet.
	prep.	except.
	adv.	only.
	n.	a given reason for not doing sth.
Butt	*n.*	thick end of a weapon.
	n.	a container *esp* for liquids.
	n.	bits of smoked cigarette.
	v.	to hit or push hard with head.
Butter	*n.*	soft milk cream.
	v.	to flatter sb.
By	*prep.*	near, along, during sth.
	prep.	used with doer to show the action performed by, also used after passive verb.
	adv.	past, before long, soon.
	pref.	*(also bye)* less important.
Cabinet	*n.*	piece of furniture with drawers or shelves.
	n.	committee of senior government ministers.
Cage	*n.*	a place of confinement.
	v.	to imprison.
Calibre (also caliber)	*n.*	the size of the hole in gun.
	n.	a person's ability.
Cam	*n.*	the part of machine for changing its movement.
	n.	a feeling of friendship & trust among people.

Can	*n.*	a container.
	v.	fire, sack.
		modal verb, be able. *(used to convey ability, strength, power, skill, permission, nature etc).*
Cape	*n.*	land touching the sea.
	n.	a cloak.
Capital	*n.*	the city from where government functions.
	n.	money.
	n.	larger letter size in writing.
	n.	top part of a pillar.
	adj.	capital punishment.
	adj.	excellent.
Carrot	*n.*	a root vegetable.
	n.	incentive.
Case	*n.*	a box, occurrence, instance, example.
		(*Grammar) a change in* noun, pronoun or adjective.
	n.	a question to be decided in court.
	n.	a matter being investigated by the police.
The case	*n.*	the true situation.
Cashew	*n.*	a kind of pumpkin.
	n.	a kind of fruit tree *(kaju).*
Cast	*n.*	mould, a throw
	v.	to look, to throw.
	v.	to shed.
Castaway	*n.*	a person whose ship has sunk.
Cast away	*v.*	to throw away
Cataract	*n.*	eye disease.
	n.	a waterfall.
Ceiling	*n.*	the inside roof of a room.
	n.	top limit.
Cell	*n.*	a small room.
	n.	plant cell.
	n.	electric battery.
Character	*n.*	mental or moral nature.
	n.	letter, sign, mark or symbol used in writing.
	n.	person or animals in a book, film etc.

Cheat	*v.*	to deceive.
	n.	a dishonest person.
Check	*n.*	stop.
	v.	to examine sth.
Cheek	*n.*	either side of the face below the eyes.
	n.	rude behaviour.
Chest	*n.*	a strong box,
	n.	the breast.
Clause	*n.*	*(grammar)* a part of sentence that has a subject & predicate.
	n.	a section of law.
Clean	*adj.*	pure, neat.
	v.	to free from dirt.
Clerical	*adj.*	related to office work.
	adj.	of clergy.
Click	*n.*	a short sharp sound.
	v.	to press button on a mouse.
Clip	*n.*	a small object for holding things together.
	n.	short part of film shown separately.
	v.	to cut sth with scissors or shears.
	v.	to fasten sth with a clip.
Close	*v.*	shut, end.
	adj.	near in space or time, almost, likely.
	adv.	not far away.
Clove	*n.*	a spice.
	n.	segment of a bulb of garlic.
	v.	*p.t.* of *cleave.* split apart.
Club	*n.*	a group of people.
	n.	a place of dancing & drinking together.
	n.	heavy stick with one end thicker than the other.
	v.	to hit with a heavy stick.
Co	*pref.*	together.
	abbre.	company.
C/o	*abbre.*	care of.

Cock	*n.*	the male hen.
	v.	to make a gun ready into position for firing.
	v.	to move a part of body.
Col	*n.*	a pass in mountains.
	abbre.	column, colonel.
Cold	*adj.*	too low temperature.
	adj.	without emotions, unfriendly.
	n.	common illness that affects nose, throat.
	adv.	suddenly or completely.
Collar	*n.*	the part of cloth around the neck.
	v.	to capture sb & hold tightly.
Comb	*n.*	an object to comb hair.
	v.	to run a comb around hair.
	v.	to search, to scour.
Complement	*n.*	sth that makes up a whole.
	v.	to complete.
	adj.	together making up whole.
Conceive	*v.*	to form an idea, to imagine.
	v.	to become pregnant.
Concern	*v.*	to affect or involve sb.
	n.	feeling of worry.
	n.	desire to protect & help sb/sth.
	n.	company or business.
Congenial	*adj.*	having same taste.
	adj.	pleasant.
Consent	*v.*	to allow
	n.	agreement.
Console	*v.*	to solace.
	n.	a panel containing controlling switches of a machine.
Content	*n.*	the things contained.
	n.	contentment.
Context	*n.*	speech or text.
	n.	a situation when sth happens.

Conveyance	*n.*	a vehicle.
	n.	the document by which property is conveyed.
Conviction	*n.*	the act of convicting.
	n.	a strong opinion or belief.
Cop	*v.*	to catch or arrest.
	n.	a police man.
Copy	*n.*	an imitation of an original.
	v.	to write exactly like the original.
Core	*n.*	hard central part of fruit.
	adj.	most important, main.
	v.	to take out the core of fruit.
Corporal	*adj.*	relating to the body.
	n.	a person of lower ranks in the army.
Country	*n.*	an area of land having its own govt. & laws.
	n.	a rural area.
Coup	*n.*	a stroke or blow.
	n.	a sudden & illegal change of government. (also coup d'etat)
Course	*v.*	to chase.
	n.	the path to move on.
	n.	a series of lessons taught in the schools.
Court	*n.*	place of legal trial.
	n.	place where games are played.
	v.	to cultivate.
	v.	to have relationship, to woo.
	adj.	different.
Cow	*n.*	the female ox.
	v.	to subdue by threats.
Crack	*v.*	to break.
	n.	a narrow opening to peep or sth to come out.
	adj.	expert.
Crane	*n.*	a tall wading bird.
	n.	a machine for lifting heavy weights.
Cricket	*n.*	a small chirping insect.
	n.	a game played with bats, ball and wickets.

Word		Meaning
Crook	*n.*	a dishonest person, criminal.
	v.	to bend finger or arm.
	adj.	sick.
Crop	*n.*	harvest.
	n.	a part of bird's throat.
	n.	a short whip used by horse riders.
Crow	*n.*	a black bird.
	v.	to boast.
Cue	*n.*	a signal for action.
	n.	a long stick used in Billiards, Pool & Snooker.
	v.	to cut short.
Cunning	*n.*	craftiness, skill.
	adj.	crafty.
Current	*adj.*	of the present.
	n.	a stream.
	n.	electric current.
Daily	*adj.*	happening everyday.
	n.	daily newspaper.
Dam	*n.*	a barrier stopping water.
	n.	the mother of some animals.
Damn	*v.*	to condemn.
	adj.	annoyed.
	v.	to show anger
	n.	not to care about.
Dash	*n.*	act of going some where quickly.
	n.	a small amount that is added to sth else.
	n.	symbol (-) used in punctuation.
	n.	sprint, race.
	v.	to rush.
	v.	to beat against a surface.
Date	*n.*	a particular day.
	n.	a sweet sticky brown fruit.
	v.	to write date.
	n.	romantic meeting.

Dead	*adj.*	not alive.
	adj.	belonging to the past.
	adj.	not working.
	adj.	numb, insensitive.
	adv.	completely, very, extremely.
	n.	people who have died.
Decree	*n.*	an official order from a ruler.
	v.	to decide, to judge.
Demo	*n.*	demonstration, display.
	pref.	meaning connected with people.
Descent	*n.*	downward slope.
	n.	ancestry.
Desert	*n.*	a desolate place.
	v.	to leave, to abandon.
	adj.	barren.
Die	*n.*	*plu* of dice used in game of chess or dice *(pasa).*
	n.	*plu* of dies. a metal block used for stamping.
	v.	to expire.
Diffuse	*v.*	to spread.
	adj.	not clear or easy to understand.
Dig	*v.*	to unearth.
	n.	a small push with fingers or elbow.
Digest	*v.*	to digest food.
	n.	a collection of short reports.
Dim	*adj.*	not bright.
	adj.	vague.
	adj.	not intelligent.
Direct	*v.*	to tell or indicate.
	adj.	frank, straight, outspoken.
Dis	*v.*	to show a lack of respect.
	pref.	the opposite of.
Dish	*n.*	food container.
	v.	to tell unpleasant things about sb.

Discount	*n.*	difference of actual rate & amount charged for sth.
	v.	not to consider sth worthy.
Do	*v.*	to execute, to perform.
	n.	a party, social event.
	abbre.	ditto.
Dodge	*n.*	a clever & dishonest trick.
	v.	to avoid doing sth.
Dog	*n.*	an animal.
	v.	to cause trouble for long time.
	v.	to follow sb closely.
Doll	*n.*	a child's toy.
	n.	used for an attractive woman.
Don	*n.*	a teacher at a university.
	v.	to put clothes etc.
Done	*adj.*	finished, completed.
	excl.	to show agreed.
	v.	do, did, done.
Doom	*n.*	death or destruction.
	v.	to make sth certain to fail, suffer.
Drive	*v.*	*drove, driven.* to run a vehicle.
	v.	to force sb to act in a particular way.
	n.	an organized effort.
	n.	a part of computer.
Drove	*v.*	*drive, drove, driven.*
	n.	a chisel.
Drug	*n.*	an illegal substance taken for pleasure & get. addicted to it.
	n.	substance used as medicine.
Drunk	*adj.*	intoxicated or having taken much alcohol.
	n.	a person who often gets drunk.
	v.	*p.p.* of *drink.*
Duck	*n.*	a common bird.
	v.	to dodge, to move body downward.

Due	*adj.*	owing, fit, claimable.
	adv.	exactly, in a straight line.
	n.	a thing that should be given to sb as a right.
Due to	*adj.*	caused by sth, because of sb/sth.
Dug	*v.*	*dig, dug, dug.*
	n.	a teat esp. of an animal.
Dully	*adj.*	dull.
	adv.	in a dull manner.
Dumb	*adj.*	stupid.
	adj.	unable to speak.
Dun	*adj.*	of grayish brown.
	n.	importunate creditor.
Duty	*n.*	tax on the things brought into a country.
	n.	moral or legal responsibility.
Dyeing	*adj.*	the process of fixing colour to a fabric.
	v.	dye + ing = dyeing.
Dying	*adj.*	about to die.
	v.	Die + ing = dying
Ear	*n.*	spike or head of a corn.
	n.	the organ of hearing.
Earth	*n.*	the world, land.
	v.	to make electrical wiring in the ground.
Eats	*v.*	*eat, eats.*
	n.	food.
Egg	*n.*	oval object produced by female bird, insect etc.
	v.	to encourage sb to do sth.
Elbow	*n.*	joint between upper & lower parts of the arm.
	v.	to push.
Elder	*adj.*	older.
	n.	small tree with white flowers & black berries.
End	*n.*	last part, aim.
	n.	a person's death.
	v.	to finish.

Engagement	*n.*	an agreement to marry sb.
	n.	an arrangement to do sth at a particular time.
	n.	process of employing sb.
Epic	*pref.*	in the sense of 'upon', 'over'.
	n.	long poem narrating heroic deeds or nation's history.
Ere	*adv & conj.*	before, sooner than.
	excl.	denoting the action done next.
Erect	*adj.*	straight.
	v.	to build sth.
	v.	to put sth up.
Espouse	*v.*	to give support to a belief, policy etc.
	v.	to marry, to adopt.
Essay	*v.*	to attempt.
	n.	a writing on a particular subject.
Ethnic	*adj.*	connected to a nation, people, race.
	n.	a person from an ethnic minority.
Even	*adv.*	at this or that exact moment.
	adj.	smooth, level & flat.
	adj.	not changing, same size, calm.
	adj.	number that can be divided by two.
Execution	*n.*	to kill sb as a legal punishment.
	n.	the act of doing a piece of work.
Exercise	*n.*	bodily exertion for developing health.
	v.	to use power, rights etc.
Exhaust	*n.*	waste gases that come out of a vehicle, engine etc.
	v.	to make sb feel very tired, wear out.
	v.	to use all of sth.
Exist	*v.*	to be in a situation.
	v.	to live.
Exit	*n.*	a way out of a public building, vehicle etc.
	v.	to go out.
	v.	to finish using a computer programme.
Expansive	*adj.*	covering a large amount of space.
	adj.	friendly & willing to talk.

Expose	*v.*	reveal.
	n.	an account of facts of situation.
Extra	*adj.*	additional.
	adv.	more than is usual.
	pref.	outside, beyond, very.
Extract	*v.*	pull out by force, remove.
	n.	a passage.
Eye	*n.*	a parts of body to see.
	n.	the hole in the end of a needle.
	n.	hook to fasten clothes.
	v.	to see.
Face	*n.*	front of head.
	v.	to confront, to be opposite.
	v.	to deal with difficult situation.
Faint	*adj.*	dim or weak.
	v.	to swoon.
Fair	*adj.*	clear, free from fault, beautiful.
	n.	a large public event.
Fall	*v.*	*p.t. fell, p.p. fallen,* to descend down.
	n.	decrease, defeat, loss of respect.
Fast	*n.*	abstinence from food.
	adj.	swift.
Fat	*adj.*	fleshy, plump.
	n.	a substance in the bodies that stores energy.
Fawn	*n.*	a young deer.
	v.	to show affection.
Feature	*n.*	characteristics.
	n.	feature film article etc.
Feel	*v.*	perceive, to know by touch.
	v.	be aware.
	n.	impression created.
Fell	*n.*	an animal's skin or hide.
	v.	*fell, felled, felled. to cut down.*

Felt	*n.*	cloth made of wool & fur.
	v.	*feel, felt, felt.*
Fiddle	*v.*	to touch things.
	v.	to change the details or figures of sth.
	n.	violin.
	n.	fraud.
File	*n.*	container for papers etc.
	n.	a collection of information on computer.
	n.	a metal tool for cutting.
	v.	to put & keep documents.
Fill	*v.*	to make full.
	n.	a full supply.
	n.	as much willing to accept.
Final	*adj.*	last, decisive.
	n.	the end.
Fine	*adj.*	very good, in good health, excellent.
	n.	payment imposed as a penalty.
Fire	*n.*	the flames after burning.
	n.	shots from guns.
	n.	strong emotions, anger etc.
Firm	*adj.*	not soft or yielding, determined.
	n.	business company.
	adv.	to believe strongly & not change mind.
Fit	*v.*	to be suitable.
	v.	to agree.
	adj.	healthy & strong.
	n.	convulsion, bout.
	n.	match.
Fix	*v.*	to settle, to set.
	n.	dilemma.
Flash	*v.*	shine brightly, move quickly.
	n.	light, signal.
	adj.	attract by expensive clothes.
Flat	*adj.*	even & smooth, dull.
	n.	set of rooms in a large building.

	adv.	spread out in level, straight position.
	n.	bright but unsteady light.
Flesh	*n.*	soft substance between bones & skin.
	v.	to add more information to a plan.
Flip	*n.*	flick.
	v.	somersault.
Flock	*n.*	animals of one kind together.
	n.	wool or cotton waste used as stuffing.
Flog	*v.*	to hang loosely.
	v.	to punish severely.
Flop	*v.*	to flutter.
	n.	a failure.
Flush	*n.*	a flow of water, toilet flush.
	adj.	having a lot of money.
	v.	to become red as embarrassed.
	n.	flock of birds.
Fly	*n.*	*(housefly)* two winged insect.
	v.	to move through air.
	adj.	sharp & cunning.
Fold	*n.*	a pen for sheep.
	v.	to double over.
For	*prep.*	in place of, instead of, for the sake of, in favour of.
	pref.	out, beyond, excess.
	conj.	expressing reason for sth.
Fore	*adj.*	situation in front.
	n.	to become important & noticed by people.
	adv.	at or towards the front of sth.
	combining form.	before, in advance.
Fore arm	*n.*	arm from the wrist to the elbow.
	v.	prepare before hand.
Forge	*n.*	smithy.
	v.	advance steadily.
Form	*n.*	shape or appearance.
	n.	class in a school.

	n.	state of health.
	n.	paper with spaces to fill in.
	v.	to shape, to construct, to develop.
Foster	*v.*	to encourage.
	n.	foster parents (not real parents).
Foul	*adj.*	dirty & smelling bad, offensive.
	n.	an act in the game that is against the rules.
Found	*v.*	*p.t. & p.p.* of *find.*
	v.	*founded, founded.* to lay the basis or foundation of.
	v.	to rely, to depend.
Founder	*n.*	one who starts an institution.
	n.	one who melts metal.
	v.	to be filled with water & sink.
Four	*adj.*	number 4.
	(cricket)	a shot that scores 4 runs.
Fret	*v.*	to wear away by friction.
	n.	irritation.
	n.	crossbar on fingerboard of a guitar.
Front	*n.*	the forepart.
	n.	battle field.
Fry	*n.*	young fish just spawned.
	v.	process of cooking.
Full	*adj.*	with no empty space, complete, busy.
	adv.	completely.
	v.	to cleanse & thicken cloth in mill.
Fuse	*v.*	to melt by heat.
	n.	electric wire.
Future	*n.*	the time to come.
	n.	one of the Tenses.
Gale	*n.*	a violent wind.
	n.	a shrub found in marshes.
Gall	*n.*	blister, sore, impudent, resentment.
	n.	bile.
	n.	oak apple.

Gas	*n.*	any substance like air.
	v.	to chat.
Gauge	*n.*	a device to measure the amount or level.
	n.	the distance between the railway line.
Genius	*n.*	intellectual person.
	n.	*(plu.* of *genii)* a demon.
German	*adj. & n.*	a native or language of Germany.
	adj.	closely related.
Get up	*v.*	to stand up, rise.
	n.	general appearance.
Gnarl	*n.*	*a* knot in wood.
	v.	growl.
Goad	*n.*	a sharp pointed stick to drive cattle.
	v.	to keep irritating.
Going	*n.*	departure.
	n.	condition of the ground in horse racing.
	v.	*go, went, gone, going.*
	adj.	going regular to the place mentioned.
Good	*adj.*	excellent, fit, valuable.
Goods	*n.*	property, wares.
Gram	*n.*	chick pea. *(chana).*
	n.	the unit of weight in metric system.
Grave	*n.*	a burial place for dead.
	n.	accent over a vowel to indicate special pronunciation.
	adj.	serious, important.
Green	*adj.*	grass coloured.
Greens	*n.*	*plu.* vegetables.
Groom	*n.*	a bridegroom.
	n.	one in charge of horses.
	v.	to smarten.
Ground	*n.*	the surface of the earth.
	v.	*grind, ground, ground.* to crush to powder.
	v.	*ground, grounded, grounded.* to establish.
	v.	to punish a child.

Gum	*n.*	firm flesh in which the teeth are set.
	n.	adhesive substance.
Gust	*n.*	a sudden blast of wind.
	n.	pleasure, taste.
Gut	*n.*	intestine, belly.
	v.	to destroy the inside or contents of a building.
	adj.	based on feelings & emotions.
Guy	*n.*	a steadying rope for tents etc.
	n.	a person of queer dress.
Hack	*v.*	to cut sth with blow.
	n.	sb who does work that is not important or original.
Hail	*interj.*	Bravo.
	v.	to call sb in order to say hello.
Hamper	*n.*	shackles.
	v.	to hinder, to impede.
Handle	*n.*	the part of an object to hold it.
	v.	to control.
Hang	*v.*	*hung, hung,* to suspend.
	v.	*hanged, hanged,* to execute.
Hanger	*n.*	a device on which to hang clothes.
	n.	a large structure for aircraft or air planes.
Harbour	*n.*	sea coast where ships can shelter.
	v.	to hide & protect.
Hard	*adj.*	solid, or stiff, difficult to bend.
	adv.	heavily.
Hash	*v.*	to chop.
	n.	the symbol (#).
Haul	*v.*	to pull with a lot of effort.
	n.	a large stolen amount of sth.
Hawk	*n.*	a bird of prey, the falcon kind.
	v.	to clear the throat noisily.
	v.	to carry about wares for sale.

Head	*n.*	the upper part of body.
	adj.	chief.
	v.	to lead.
	n.	a horse for ordinary riding.
Heap	*n.*	an untidy pile of sth.
	n.	a lot of sth.
	excl.	show approval
Heart	*n.*	an organ that pumps blood.
	n.	vital centre & source of one's being.
Heat	*n.*	hotness.
	v.	to make hot.
Heel	*n.*	back part of the foot below the ankle.
	n.	unpleasant man.
Hide	*n.*	the skin of a beast.
	v.	to keep out of sight.
High	*n.*	an elevated place.
	adj.	towering.
	adv.	far up.
Hind	*n.*	a female deer, a rustic.
	adj.	placed at the back.
Hip	*n.*	the area at either side of the body between the top
	n.	of the leg & waist.
	adj.	following the fashionable clothes, music etc.
Hit	*v.*	to strike with a blow.
	n.	a person or thing that is very popular.
Hoard	*n.*	stock, store.
	v.	to lay up.
Hoop	*v.*	to make a wheezy sound.
	n.	a large ring of plastic, wood or iron.
Hop	*n.*	a tall climbing plant with bitter cones.
	n.	short journey.
	v.	to move by jumping.
Hope	*n.*	expectation.
	v.	to anticipate.

Hose	*n.*	flexible pipe for conveying liquids.
	n.	stockings, socks & tights.
Host	*n.*	person who entertains guests in his own home.
	n.	an anchor of a programme.
	n.	large number.
	v.	to compere a show.
Hug	*v.*	to embrace.
	n.	a close embrace.
Impress	*n.*	a stamp, a seal.
	v.	to influence.
Interest	*n.*	wanting to know more.
	n.	hobby.
	n.	the extra money paid back on the borrowed money.
Intimate	*v.*	to inform.
	adj.	very close or friendly.
Iron	*n.*	hard strong metal.
	v.	to press clothes.
	v.	to get rid of any problem.
	adj.	very strong, determined.
Issue	*n.*	an important topic of discussion.
	n.	regular series of magazines, news papers.
	n.	own children.
	n.	problem or worry that sb has with sth.
	v.	to give sth to sb.
	v.	to make sth known.
Keel	*n.*	the long piece of wood or steel along the bottom of ship.
	v.	to capsize.
Keen	*adj.*	having a sharp edge, acute.
	adj.	eager.
	v.	to lament for dead.
Kid	*n.*	a young goat.
	n.	small tub.
Kill	*n.*	murder, assassinate, a prey.
	v.	to slay.

Killing	*n.*	murder.
	adj.	exhausting.
Kind	*n.*	race, class, variety.
	adj.	sympathetic, considerate.
	adj.	*kind, kinder, kindest.*
Kite	*n.*	a bird of prey of the hawk family.
	n.	a paper toy for flying in the air.
Knave	*n.*	a clever trickster.
	n.	a playing card depicting jokester.
Knot	*n.*	a join made by two pieces of strings.
	n.	a way of twisting hair.
	n.	a hard round spot in piece of wood.
	n.	a tight hard feeling in stomach, throat etc.
	n.	unit for measuring speed of boat & aircraft.
	v.	to fasten with knot.
Labour	*n.*	exertion of the body or mind.
	n.	childbirth.
	v.	to struggle or do hard work.
Lac	*n.*	lakh.
	n.	a resinous substance.
Lamb	*n.*	a young sheep
	n.	an innocent person.
Land	*n.*	the dry part of earth.
	v.	to come down to the ground.
	v.	to take off.
Lash	*n.*	eyelash, sharp blow with a whip.
	v.	fasten or bind tightly with cord etc.
Last	*det.*	Final.
	adv.	at the end.
	v.	to continue for a particular period of time.
	n.	model used to repair or make shoes.
Late	*adj.*	near the end of a period of time.
	adv.	after the expected, arranged or usual time.
	adj.	used before the name of dead person.

Lay	*n.*	a narrative poem, song.
	v.	*p.t.* of lie. *lie, lay, lain.* to place.
	adj.	unprofessional.
	v.	*laid, laid.* to set, to lay eggs.
	n.	a partner in sex.
Leap	*v.*	to spring up.
	n.	a jump.
Learned	*v.*	*learn, learned, learned.* (also *learn, learnt, earnt)* to acquire knowledge.
	v.	memorize.
	adj.	having great knowledge.
Leave	*n.*	permission to go somewhere.
	v.	*leave, left, left.* to depart from.
Leaves	*plu.*	of *leaf.*
Left	*v.*	*p.t. & p.p.* of *leave.*
	adj.	opposite of right.
Lent	*v.*	*p.t. & p.p.* of *lend.*
	n.	fast before Easter.
Less	*det.*	a smaller amount of.
	adv.	not so much.
	prep.	minus.
	suff.	without.
Let	*v.*	to give sb permission to do sth.
	v.	to allow sb to use a room etc. in return of payment.
	aux.	to permit, to allow.
	v.	to lease.
	n.	impediment, prohibition.
	suff.	used in sense of small.
Letter	*n.*	small or capital letter of alphabet.
	n.	written message addressed to sb.
Level	*n.*	a particular standard or quality.
	adj.	flat, equal.
	v.	to raze.
Levy	*v.*	to impose, to raise
	n.	tax paid to government.

Lie	*n.*	untruth.
	v.	*lie, lied, lied.* to tell a lie, to deceive.
	v.	*lie, lay, lain.* to take rest.
Light	*n.*	a lamp.
	adj.	bright.
	adj.	not heavy.
Lighten	*v.*	to lessen.
	v.	to cheer.
	v.	to make brighter.
Like	*adj.*	similar, equal.
	adj.	pleasing.
	v.	be fond of, adore, to approve.
	conj.	in the same way as, as if.
	n.	better, more acceptable.
	combining form.	similar to, typical of.
List	*n.*	a catalogue, the edge of cloth.
	v.	to enlist.
	v.	to desire, to listen, lean.
Live	*v.*	to dwell, to have life.
	adj.	alive, active, living, not dead.
	adv.	broadcast of a happening.
Lo	*interj.*	look, behold.
	excl.	used to say when surprised.
Loaf	*n.*	a separate piece of bread.
	v.	to hang about/around.
Long	*adj.*	large.
	adv.	for or during a long time.
	v.	to desire, to yearn.
	abbre.	longitude.
Loot	*v.*	to steal things.
	n.	booty.
Lost	*adj.*	unable to find way.
	v.	*lose, lost, lost.*
Lot	*n.*	area of land.
	n.	destiny.

	n.	items to be sold.
	v.	to put lottery.
Love	*n.*	affection.
	n.	a score of zero in tennis.
	v.	feel affection.
Low	*adj.*	not high, not bright.
	adv.	near the bottom of sth.
	n.	a low figure.
	v.	a sound of cow, moo.
Magazine	*n.*	a military supply depot or a ware house.
	n.	a periodical publication.
Maiden	*n.*	a girl.
	adj.	unmarried or virgin.
Mail	*n.*	letters & parcels sent by post.
	v.	to cloth an armour, to post.
Mandatory	*n.*	who gets a mandate addressed.
	adj.	compulsory to be done.
Manner	*n.*	a method of doing sth.
Manners	*n.*	conduct.
March	*n.*	a boundary of a country.
	n.	the third month of the year.
	v.	to walk like a soldier.
Mark	*v.*	to indicate.
	v.	to celebrate.
	v.	to give marks to the students.
	n.	a spot or cut mark.
	n.	a symbol, sign, a target.
Maroon	*adj.*	dark brownish red in colour.
	n.	large fire works.
	v.	to confine in a place, strand.
Mars	*n.*	the God of war.
	n.	a red planet.
Mash	*n.*	a warm food for horses.
	v.	to crush food into soft mass.

Mask	*n.*	covering to hide or protect face.
	v.	to disguise.
Mass	*n.*	lots, a large number or amount of sth.
	n.	what sth contains.
	v.	to gather in large number.
Master	*n.*	person in control.
	adj.	over all or controlling.
	v.	to get knowledge & skill in, overcome.
Match	*n.*	stick for lighting fire.
	n.	sports events.
	n.	an equal.
	n.	a marriage partner.
	v.	be the same, similar.
Mate	*n.*	friend.
	v.	*(animal & birds)* to have sex.
May	*modal*	*aux.* expressing possibility, permission, wish, pray etc.
	n.	the fifth month of the year.
Mean	*adj.*	base, mediocre.
	adj.	not generous.
	v.	*mean, meant, meant.* what one wants to say.
	n.	average *(arithmetic & geometric mean).*
Mean while	*adv.*	during this time.
	n.	for a short period of time.
Measure	*n.*	size, unit.
	v.	to assess.
Meet	*v.*	*meet, met, met.* come into contact with.
	adj.	fit or suitable.
Mercury	*n.*	the smallest planet in the solar system.
	n.	a chemical element.
Mere	*n.*	a pond or lake.
	adj.	only this and nothing else.
Mess	*n.*	disorder.
	n.	room to take meal together.

Middle	*adj.*	intermediate.
	n.	the centre of anything.
Milk	*n.*	white fluid secreted by females.
	v.	to obtain milk from female animals.
Mind	*n.*	intellect, brain.
	v.	to look after.
	v.	to feel upset or annoyed.
Mine	*poss.*	*pron.* belonging to me.
	n.	from where minerals are obtained.
	v.	to dig mine.
Mint	*n.*	a plant with dark green leaves *(podina).*
	n.	a place where money is made.
A mint	*n.*	a large amount of money.
Minute	*n.*	sixty seconds.
	adj.	precise, tiny, very small.
	n.	record of decisions taken in a meeting.
	n.	we measure angles in minutes.
Miss	*v.*	failure to hit.
	v.	escape.
	n.	a young unmarried girl.
Mole	*n.*	small dark raised spot on the skin.
	n.	small burrowing mammal.
	n.	a protected harbour.
	n.	unit of amount of substance.
Monitor	*n.*	head boy in the class.
	v.	to supervise.
	n.	a television or computer screen.
Mono	*n.*	a system of recording.
		combining form. one, single.
Moon	*n.*	a celestial body that revolve round the earth.
	v.	to wander aimlessly or dreamily.
Mop	*n.*	an object to clean floors.
	n.	a mass of thick hair.

More	*adj.*	greater in quantity.
Mores	*n.*	social behaviour.
Most	*det, pron.*	the largest number or amount.
		s*uperlative* of much, a lot of, many.
	adv.	to the greatest degree.
	suff.	the furthest.
Movement	*n.*	a group of people working for an aim.
	n.	changing position.
Mug	*n.*	a drinking vessel with handle.
	n.	human face, mouth.
Mull	*n.*	a soft muslin.
	v.	to think over, consider.
	v.	to heat wine with spices & sugar.
Nail	*n.*	horny growth at the tip of fingers & toes.
	n.	a sharp metal used as peg.
	v.	to fix together with nails.
Nature	*n.*	all the creation on the earth.
	n.	main features of sth.
	n.	real character of sb.
Neat	*adj.*	tidy.
	n.	ox, cow or bull.
Net	*n.*	a web made by thread or wire tied together.
	n.	internet.
	v.	score.
Noble	*adj.*	loft, great, splendid.
	n.	a person of high social rank.
Note	*n.*	a short piece of writing as reminder.
	n.	a piece of paper money.
	n.	a single sound of a particular length & pitch *(music).*
	v.	jot down.
Novel	*adj.*	new, peculiar, unusual.
	n.	a fiction, imaginary long story book.
Nut	*n.*	a small hard fruit.
	n.	a small piece of metal with a hole.
Nuts	*adj.*	crazy.

Object	*n.*	a thing or commodity.
	n.	an aim or purpose.
	v.	to oppose, protest.
		(grammar). thing that is affected by the action of the verb.
Odd	*adj.*	not even.
Odds	*n.*	*plu.* inequality.
Operation	*n.*	cutting open a part of body as a treatment.
	n.	military or organized activity.
Or	*conj.*	*& prep.* introducing an alternative.
	suff.	a person or thing that.
Oral	*adj.*	to do with the mouth.
	n.	a spoken exam.
Order	*n.*	class, grade, rank.
	n.	command.
	n.	method.
	n.	public tranquility.
Out	*adv, prep.*	away from the inside.
	n.	a way of avoiding having to do sth.
	v.	to force sb to quit.
	adj.	absent, no longer secret.
	pref.	further, outside, away from.
Over	*adj.*	above, more, remaining
	prep.	resting on the surface of sb/sth & covering them.
	n.	in cricket, six balls bowled.
	pref.	more than usual, too much, completely.
Owing	*adj.*	money that has not been paid yet.
Owing to	*prep.*	because of.
Own	*n.*	of oneself.
	v.	to possess, to have sth.
Pale	*n.*	stake, enclosure.
	adj.	dim.
Pall	*n.*	a black cloth laid over coffin at a funeral.
	v.	to make or become tedious.

Palm	*n.*	the inner surface of the hand.
	n.	a branchless tropical tree *(taad).*
	v.	to conceal in palm.
Pan	*n.*	a broad pot used in cooking.
	pref.	denoting total.
	combining form.	including all of sth.
Panel	*n.*	a provision of metal that is part of the outer frame.
	n.	group of specialists.
Para	*pref.*	denoting beside, beyond or contrary to.
	n.	short form of paragraph.
Parent	*n.*	a person's father or mother.
Parents	*n.*	a person's father & mother.
Park	*n.*	an area of public land.
	v.	to park vehicle.
Part	*n.*	portion, share, lot.
	v.	to divide.
Pass	*v.*	to go, to get through.
	n.	a narrow way through a mountain range.
	n.	a permission card.
	n.	a critical stage or situation.
Patient	*adj.*	showing patience.
	n.	a sick person in the hospital.
Patho	*combining form.*	connected with disease.
Pathos	*n.*	feelings of pity or sadness.
Pen	*n.*	a device for writing with ink.
	n.	small shelter for domestic animals.
	n.	female swan.
Per	*pref.*	all over, completely, very.
	prep.	by means of, for every.
Perch	*n.*	a fresh water fish.
	n.	sitting place for birds.
Period	*n.*	a particular length of time.
	n.	time schedule divided in schools.

	n.	the menstruating of women.
	adv.	full stop (.) a punctuation mark.
Person	*n.*	human being.
	Grammar	three persons of pronoun.
Photo	*n.*	photograph.
		combining form connected with light, photography.
Pick	*n.*	a sharp pointed tool.
	v.	to dig, to uplift.
Pie	*n.*	a mag pie, species of wood pecker.
	n.	fruit baked in a dish.
	n.	a printing type indiscriminately mixed.
	n.	a coin, small amount.
Pile	*n.*	a head, heap.
Piles	*n.*	a disease, hemorrhoids.
Pill	*n.*	small round medicine to swallow.
	v.	to become covered in very small balls of fibre.
Pin	*n.*	a piece of small wire with pointed end.
	v.	to attach or fasten sth onto another.
PIN	*abbre.*	Postal Index Number, or Personal Identification number.
Pine	*n.*	an evergreen tree having cones.
	v.	to become feeble due to sickness or sorrow.
Plain	*adj.*	clear, simple, easy.
	n.	a large area of flat land.
	v.	to yearn.
Plant	*n.*	a living thing growing in the earth having stem,
	n.	leaves & roots.
	n.	a factory, machinery.
	v.	to put sth strongly in a place.
	v.	to plant tree.
Play	*v.*	to take part in game.
	n.	a drama.
Please	*v.*	to make happy or to satisfy.
		adv & interj. expressing polite request.

Pole	*n.*	a long stick set straight in the ground.
	n.	north or south poles.
Polish	*v.*	to make smooth & glossy.
	n.	substance to make surface shiny.
	n.	citizen of Poland.
Pool	*n.*	a small still water area.
	n.	a game played by two.
	v.	to gather sth.
Pop	*n.*	a sudden explosive sound.
	n.	modern popular music.
Pose	*v.*	to create a threat, problem.
	v.	to give position for getting photographed.
Post	*n.*	a structure of wood or metal set upright as a support.
	n.	an official organization for mailing letters.
	n.	a job, position.
	v.	to mail letters etc.
Pound	*v.*	to make into powder.
	n.	an enclosure for stray cattle.
	n.	a measure of weight.
Practice	*n.*	habitual action, custom.
	n.	when doctors or lawyers work it is called practice.
Premier	*adj.*	most important.
	n.	used for Prime Minister.
Present	*adj.*	existing now, actual.
	n.	a gift.
	v.	to give sth to sb.
Presents	*n.*	writing in a legal documents.
Pride	*n.*	noble self esteem, arrogance.
	n.	a group of lions.
Primer	*n.*	a type of paint.
	n.	a book that contains basic instructions.
	n.	elementary book for small children.
Principal	*adj.*	most important, chief.
	n.	head of a school or college.
	n.	sum of money originally borrowed or lent.

Prior	*n.*	a monk.
	adj.	previous.
Prize	*n.*	a reward.
	adj.	treasure.
Project	*n.*	planned work, scheme.
	n.	set of aims.
	n.	careful study of any topic.
	v.	to forecast.
	v.	to throw forward.
Pulse	*n.*	breathing artery.
	n.	seed of beans & cereals.
Quack	*n.*	the sound a duck makes.
	n.	a person practicing medicine without proper. knowledge or skill of it.
Quarry	*n.*	mines.
	n.	prey.
Quarter	*n.*	one of four parts.
	n.	a persons deemed as a source of help.
	n.	rooms to live in.
	n.	mercy.
Query	*n.*	an enquiry about sth.
	n.	a question mark to show why the task has not been accomplished.
Quiver	*n.*	a case for arrows.
	v.	to shiver.
Race	*n.*	trial of speed.
	n.	tribe, family, breed.
	n.	a breed type of animal or plants.
Rad	*adj.*	very good.
	n.	a unit for measuring the effects of Radiation.
Rag	*n.*	torn cloth.
	v.	to tease.
Ragged	*adj.*	old & torn, shabby.
	adj.	very tired.

Rail	*v.*	to use harsh or abusive language.
	n.	train.
	v.	to complain angrily about sth.
Ram	*n.*	a male sheep.
	v.	to push sth somewhere with force.
RAM	*n.*	*abbre.* Random Access Memory.
Rape	*v.*	to carry away by force.
	n.	sexual intercourse with a woman against her will.
	n.	turnip like plant.
Rapid	*adj.*	fast.
Rapids	*n.*	a dangerous part of a river.
Rash	*n.*	showing red spots on a person's skin.
	n.	a lot of sth.
	adj.	impulsive, reckless.
Rat	*n.*	a mouse.
Rats	*excl.*	used to show anger.
Rate	*n.*	proportion, tax, cost.
	n.	measurement of the speed.
	v.	rank, merit.
Reach	*v.*	to arrive, achieve aim.
	n.	the distance covered.
Reading	*n.*	when sb reads.
	n.	reading material like books, articles.
	n.	interpretation.
	n.	record on a meter.
	n.	when a bill is discussed in the parliament.
	v.	*read, read, read, reading.*
Rear	*n.*	the hind most part.
	v.	to raise, to build, to breed, to educate.
Reel	*n.*	a dance, a bobbin.
	n.	to move in a very unsteady way.
	n.	a reel together with the film.
	v.	stagger.
Refrain	*v.*	desist from.
	n.	an oft repeated complaint.
	n.	chorus.

Region	*n.*	tract of land.
	n.	a part of the body, usually one that has a particular character or problem.
Register	*n.*	a book of record.
	n.	musical compass.
	v.	to notice sth.
	v.	to record name in the list.
Relay	*n.*	relay race.
	v.	to broadcast a programme.
Rent	*n.*	amount paid for use of land, room etc.
	n.	a tear or hole in a material.
Repent	*adj.*	creeping as a plant.
	adj.	to regret.
Resent	*v.*	to feel bitter or angry about sth.
	v.	sent again.
Rest	*v.*	to stop doing, to sleep.
	n.	repose, leisure.
	n.	remainder.
Resume	*v.*	to take up again.
	n.	summary, bio-data, epitome, curriculum vitae.
Retort	*v.*	to retaliate.
	n.	a container for distilling substances.
Right	*adj.*	correct, proper.
	n.	legal claim to have sth.
	n.	*opp* of left *(side) and wrong.*
	v.	return to position.
Ring	*n.*	circular band worn on the finger.
	n.	a small hoop.
	v.	to make sound of bell.
Rise	*n.*	an increase.
	v.	*rose, risen.* get up, to stand up.
	v.	appearing of sun or moon over horizon.
River	*n.*	a stream of water.
	n.	one that rives *(tears).*

Rock	*v.*	to move backward or forward.
	n.	a large mass of stony material.
Rode	*v.*	*p.t.* of *ride.*
	v.	to fly in the evening.
Room	*n.*	a chamber to live in.
	v.	to rent a room somewhere.
Rose	*v.*	*rise, rose, risen.* to stand up
	n.	a beautiful flower.
	adj.	pink in colour.
Round	*adj.*	circular, whole.
	adv.	on all sides, about, here & there.
	prep.	in a circle.
	n.	a globe, circle.
	v.	to turn on.
Row	*n.*	line, rank.
	v.	to ferry boat.
Ruler	*n.*	one who rules or governs.
	n.	a straight strip for measuring or drawing.
Run	*v.*	to walk with fast steps.
	n.	a tour.
	n.	point scored in game of cricket.
Rush	*v.*	to run fast.
	n.	sudden & busy movement.
	n.	a plant that generally grows near marsh.
Rut	*n.*	the track of wheel.
	n.	the copulation of animals.
Sack	*n.*	a large bag of coarse cloth.
	v.	to dismiss from job, fire.
Safe	*n.*	cupboard to keep valuables.
	adj.	unharmed, secure.
Sage	*n.*	an aromatic herb used in cooking.
	n.	a wise person.
Sail	*n.*	piece of canvas used in ships.
	v.	to travel by sea.

Sans	*prep.*	without.
	adv.	until now.
Sap	*n.*	moisture or liquid in plants.
	v.	undermine, weaken.
Saw	*n.*	a cutting tool with toothed edge.
	n.	saying, maxim.
	v.	*p.t. sawed, p.p. sawn, sawed,* to use a saw to cut sth.
	v.	*see, saw, seen.*
Saying	*v.*	*say, said, said, saying.*
	n.	adage, rumour.
Scape	*v.*	to escape.
	n.	an invasion.
	n.	leafless flower stalk.
		combining form. a view or scene of.
Scarce	*adj.*	available in small quantity.
	adv.	only just, almost not.
Scene	*n.*	a performance on the stage.
	n.	view.
Scent	*n.*	smell, fragrance.
	v.	to perceive by smell.
School	*n.*	where children learn.
	n.	group of writers, artists.
	n.	a large number of fish.
	v.	to train, to educate.
Score	*n.*	number won, an incision.
	v.	to succeed, to make a cut or mark on a surface.
Scrape	*v.*	to make grating noise.
	n.	difficult situation.
Seal	*n.*	a sea animal.
	v.	to put a seal.
	v.	to close sth.
Sear	*v.*	scorch.
	adj.	very sharp.
Second	*n.*	a minute has 60 seconds.
	adj.	immediately after the first, inferior.

See	*v.*	to behold, to visit, to witness.
	n.	the office of a Bishop.
Self	*n.*	one's individual person.
	adj.	absorbed by one's own interest.
	pref.	of or by oneself or itself, automatically.
Sense	*n.*	one of the five powers *(sight, hearing, smell, taste. & touch.)*
	n.	normal state of mind.
	n.	meaning.
	v.	to feel, to guess.
	v.	become aware.
Sentence	*n.*	a group of meaningful words that makes a sense.
	n.	the punishment ordered by a court.
Sept	*n.*	a clan.
	abbre.	September.
	pref.	in the sense of seven.
Serial	*adj.*	of or in a series.
	n.	a television or radio serial.
Set	*n.*	group.
	n.	(also sett) home of badger.
	v.	to put in a position.
	v.	to fix.
	v.	to compose.
	v.	to sink below horizon (sun, moon etc).
	adj.	fixed, firm.
Sex	*n.*	character of being male or female, sexual activity.
		combining form. six.
Shake	*v.*	to move from firmness.
	n.	a drink as milkshake.
Sham	*v.*	to pretend.
	n.	thing or person that is not genuine.
Share	*v.*	divide among people.
	n.	portion or claim as one's due.
	n.	blade of a plough.

Shaving	*v.*	*shave, shaving.*
Shavings	*n.*	thin pieces cut from wood.
She	*pron.*	the *opp* of *he.*
	n.	a female animal.
S/he	*pron.*	used when it is not clear that the subject is *she* or *he.*
Sheaf	*n.*	a bundle of papers tied together.
	n.	a bunch of cut stalks of grain.
Shear	*v.*	*sheared, shorn.* to cut wool of a sheep.
Shears	*n.*	a garden scissors.
Shed	*v.*	to let or have fall of.
	n.	roofed shelter.
Sheer	*adj.*	pure, mere.
	v.	to deviate from proper course.
Sheet	*n.*	a piece of linen or metal.
	n.	rope for controlling the position of sail.
Shell	*n.*	a hard outer covering.
	n.	a frail boat.
	v.	to bombard.
Shift	*v.*	to move.
	v.	get rid of.
	n.	a period of time worked.
	n.	a system on a computer keyboard.
Shingle	*n.*	small flat wood to cover the roof.
	v.	to cut the hair very close.
Ship	*n.*	a vessel.
	v.	to be available to be bought.
	suff.	the state or quality of.
Shoal	*n.*	small hill of sand bank.
	v.	to crowd, to become shallow.
Shoe	*n.*	covering for the foot.
	n.	a part of a brake.
Short	*adj, adv & noun.*	not long or tall.
Shorts	*n.*	short trousers.

Shoulder	*n.*	parts of the body at the top of each arm & neck.
	v.	to accept the responsibility for sth.
Shout	*v.*	to say loudly.
	n.	a loud cry.
Show	*v.*	to display.
	n.	an exhibition, display.
Shower	*n.*	a brief fall of rain or snow.
	v.	to drop a lot of small things onto sb.
Sick	*adj.*	ill.
	v.	to vomit.
Sine	*n.*	*(abbre- sin)* the ratio of the length of side opposite
	n.	one of the angles in a right angled triangle.
	prep.	without.
Singular	*n.*	*opp* of *plural.*
	adj.	outstanding.
	adj.	eccentric.
Sitting	*n.*	sittings of a court or parliament.
	v.	*sit, sat, sat, sitting.*
Sky	*n.*	the space above the earth.
	v.	*skied, skied.* to hit a ball very high into the air.
Slack	*adj.*	loose slow sluggish.
	n.	a dull period.
	v.	to work less hard than usual.
Slop	*n.*	a policeman.
	n.	dirty water of a household.
Slops	*n.*	trousers.
Slough	*n.*	muddy place.
	n.	the cast skin of serpent.
Slow	*adj.*	not fast, sluggish.
	adv.	slowly.
	v.	to make less active.
Sober	*adj.*	not drunk.
	adj.	serious & sensible.

Sock	*n.*	a light stocking.
	n.	plough share.
Soil	*n.*	the top layer of the earth.
	n.	a country, an area of land.
	v.	to make sth dirty.
Soldier	*n.*	military man.
	v.	to continue with the task.
Sole	*n.*	the base of shoes, bottom of a thing.
	adj.	only, single.
Some	*adj.*	certain, indefinite amount or number.
	adv.	approximately.
Some/Som	*suff.*	productive of, likely to.
Some time	*adv.*	for a portion of time.
	adv.	occasionally.
Soothe	*v.*	to calm
	v.	firmly fixed on truth.
Sore	*adj.*	painful, sad, annoyed.
	n.	wound.
	adv.	severely, greatly.
Sound	*adj.*	whole or healthy.
	n.	noise.
	n.	a strait, the air bladder of a fish.
Sour	*adj.*	having a pungent taste.
	adj.	not cheerful.
Sow	*v.*	to scatter seed in the ground.
	v.	to spread feelings in sb's mind.
	n.	a female pig.
Space	*n.*	empty area, room.
	n.	outside earth's atmosphere.
	n.	a period of time.
	n.	the part of a line, page that is empty.
	v.	to arrange things with regular spaces between them.
Spectacle	*n.*	sight, scene.
Spectacles	*n.*	eye glasses.

Spell	*n.*	charm, fascination.
	v.	to tell the spelling of word.
	n.	period.
Spirit	*n.*	mind, feelings & character together.
	n.	courage, determination.
	n.	soul, a ghost.
Spoke	*p.t.*	*&p.p.* of *speak.*
	n.	bars inside hub of a wheel.
	n.	strong alcoholic drink.
Spring	*v.*	to jump, to leap.
	n.	sudden movement.
	n.	a source of water.
	n.	a season.
Square	*n.*	figure with four equal sides and four right angles.
	n.	an open space in a town.
	n.	the product of a number multiplied by itself.
	adv.	directly.
Stable	*adj.*	firm, steady.
	n.	where horses live.
Staff	*n.*	a stick, support.
	n.	employees of an organization.
Stake	*n.*	a pointed stick or post driven into the ground.
	n.	money wagered.
	v.	to support, to risk money, to bet.
The stake	*n.*	a post to punish criminals.
Stale	*adj.*	not fresh.
	n.	a decoy bird.
Stalk	*n.*	the stem of a plant.
	n.	a high proud walk.
Stand	*v.*	to get up, to endure.
	n.	a stationary position.
State	*n.*	condition, rank.
	n.	free civil community.
	v.	to write or say sth.

Steer	*n.*	a young ox.
	v.	to direct the course of a ship etc.
Stem	*n.*	long part of plant above ground.
	v.	to stop flowing from spreading.
Stern	*adj.*	strict, harsh.
	n.	the hind part of ship or boat.
Stick	*n.*	a rod, a staff.
	v.	to stab, to adhere.
Still	*adj.*	silent, motionless.
	adv.	yet, always, notwithstanding,
	n.	photograph.
	n.	equipment used for making alcoholic drink.
Stock	*n.*	an available supply of goods.
Stocks	*n.*	a wooden structure used in the past to punish the criminals.
Stoop	*v.*	to bend down.
	n.	a platform, a porch.
Strait	*adj.*	narrow, strict, difficult.
	n.	a narrow area of sea connecting larger sea.
Strand	*n.*	shore of sea.
	n.	a single thin piece of thread etc.
	v.	to confine sb in a place.
Stray	*v.*	to move away from a place.
	adj.	*(animals)* having no home.
Strike	*v.*	to hit, to give blow.
	v.	to come an idea in mind.
	v.	*&* *n.* to protest & refuse to work.
	v.	chime.
	n.	in cricket, batsman who is on strike.
Strip	*v.*	to undress, dismantle.
	n.	long piece of paper, metal, cloth etc.
Stroke	*n.*	a blow, a sudden attack.
	v.	to pass the hand gently along.

Stuff	*n.*	a material.
	v.	to fill in.
Sub	*pref.*	below less than, under.
	n.	subordinate,
	abbre.	of *subject..*
	n.	substitute.
Subject	*n.*	a theme or topic.
	n.	subjects in the school, college (*grammar*) that performs the action of the verb.
	n.	a citizen.
	adj.	likely to be affected by sth.
	v.	to subdue, to subordinate.
Sum	*n.*	total, gist.
	v.	to bring together into one whole.
Summon	*v.*	to call.
Summons	*n.*	an order to appear in a court.
Summary	*n.*	an abstract or brief account.
	adj.	of the summer.
Sun	*n.*	the brightest celestial body.
	v.	to bask in the sun.
Super	*pref.*	in the sense of above beyond.
	adj.	excellent.
	n.	a supernumerary.
	adj.	capable of being overcome.
Swallow	*v.*	to drink.
	n.	a small bird *(avabeel).*
Swing	*v.*	to move to & fro.
	v.	change mood.
	n.	a seat for swinging on.
Tail	*n.*	an appendage of an animal.
	n.	ownership limited to a person or his heirs.
Talk	*v.*	to converse.
	n.	conversation.
Tall	*adj.*	high in stature.
	adv.	boastfully.

Toll	*n.*	a tax paid for using road, bridge etc.
	n.	the death bell.
	v.	to make metal hard.
Tap	*n.*	a device to control the water flow, a light blow.
	v.	to strike lightly.
Tape	*n.*	a sound recorder.
	v.	to record sth.
Tare	*n.*	harmful weeds among corn.
	n.	allowance for weight of package of goods.
Taste	*n.*	liking, choice.
	v.	to detect the flavour by taste.
Test	*n.*	witness.
	n.	an examination.
	v.	to attest & date.
	v.	to make a will.
	n.	trial.
Tear	*v.*	to rend, to divide.
	n.	a drop of fluid from eye.
Tee	*n.*	a metallic umbrella crowning *pagoda.*
	n.	a flat area on a golf course.
Teen	*n.*	grief, misfortune.
Teens	*n.*	a period of life between 13 to 19 years, adolescence.
Temple	*n.*	a building where Hindu worship.
	n.	the space between the forehead & the ear.
Tender	*n.*	who takes care of another.
	v.	to make offer of.
	adj.	delicate, fragile.
Tense	*adj.*	stretched, tight, rigid, uneasy.
	n.	form of verb indicating time.
	v.	to tense muscles.
Term	*n.*	word used to say sth.
	n.	a period of time.
Tide	*n.*	rise & fall of sea.
	v.	to help sb in difficulty.

Tidy	*adj.*	arranged neatly & orderly.
	adj.	considerable amount.
	v.	to make sth look neat.
	n.	container for putting small objects.
Till	*n.*	money box in a shop.
	v.	to cultivate *(land).*
	prep.	to the time of, until.
	conj.	to the time that.
	n.	cash register.
Tire	*n.*	a battery.
	n.	a head dress.
	v.	to become weary.
Ton	*n.*	metric measure of weight 1000 kg.
	n.	prevailing fashion or mode.
Tone	*n.*	the pitch of vocal or musical sound.
	n.	a shade of colour.
	n.	the pitch.
	v.	to make muscles skin firmer & stronger.
Trail	*v.*	to draw along behind, to hunt.
	n.	a route followed for a particular purpose.
Train	*n.*	a railway.
	n.	a number of people or animal in a line.
	v.	to teach, to educate.
Trip	*n.*	a journey.
	v.	to fall or almost fall.
	v.	to release a switch etc.
Trunk	*n.*	the thick main stem of a tree.
	n.	the long nose of an elephant.
	n.	the main part of human body apart from head, arms & legs.
Trunks	*n.*	swimming trunk.
Try	*n.*	attempt.
	v.	to make an effort to sth.
Turn	*v.*	to divert, to change.
	n.	revolution, new trend.
	n.	opportunity.

Under	*prep.*	beneath, below, less than.
	adj.	lower, underneath.
	pref.	below, beneath, not enough.
Very	*adj.*	true, real, actual.
	adv.	in a high degree, absolutely, truly.
Vessel	*n.*	a utensil, container.
	n.	a ship or boat.
Vest	*n.*	a waist coat.
	v.	to belong to sb/sth legally.
Vet	*n.*	veterinary surgeon.
	v.	to screen.
View	*n.*	an opinion.
	n.	scene.
	n.	a way of thinking about sth.
	v.	to look at sth, to watch.
Wag	*n.*	a moving to & fro.
	v.	to shake tail, finger.
	n.	joker.
Want	*v.*	to have a desire or wish, need.
	n.	lack, being poor.
Ward	*n.*	a minor under a guardian.
	v.	to protect.
	suff.	towards a direction.
Waste	*adj.*	uncultivated, barren, discarded.
	v.	to devastate, to misuse
Watch	*v.*	to look..
	n.	a small clock worn on wrist.
Wave	*n.*	movement in the sea water.
	v.	to move hand in the air.
Way	*n.*	method or manner of doing sth.
	n.	route or road, direction.
	adv.	very far, by a large amount.

Weed	*n.*	unwanted plants which grow themselves amid
	n.	crops.
Weeds	*n.*	mourning dress of a widow.
Weld	*v.*	to hammer into union.
	n.	a plant affording a yellow
Well	*adv.*	in a good, right or acceptable way.
	adj.	in good health.
	excl.	used to express surprise, anger or relief.
	n.	deep hole in ground to obtain water.
Whang	*n.*	leathern thong.
	n.	a blow, a bang.
	v.	to cut in large slices, to flog.
While	*conj.*	when.
	n.	a period of time.
	v.	to spend time in a pleasant, lazy way.
Whole	*adj.*	healthy, entire
	n.	sum.
Wig	*n.*	artificial head of hair.
	v.	to scold.
Will	*modal verb.*	used in future tense with second &
	n.	third person & with first person to express
	n.	determination, promise, threat etc.
	n.	legal document assigning the claim over property after death.
	v.	to wish, to extend.
Wind	*v.*	*p.t. & p.p. wound* to turn, to coil.
	v.	to turn a handle several times.
	n.	air.
	n.	group of musical instruments in an orchestra.
	v.	to wrap around sth.
Wise	*adj.*	having wisdom, sagacious.
	n.	mode, manner.
Won't	*contraction*	of will not.
Wont	*n.*	custom, habit.
	adj.	accustomed.

Wood	*n.*	a hard material out of tree.
Woods	*n.*	forest.
	n.	a golf club.
Worth	*n.*	value, price.
	v.	to be, all.
Would	*v.*	*modal verb. p.t.* of *will* used to express polite request, past habit, unreal condition. etc.
	adj.	tending to be.
Wound	*n.*	hurt, damage, pain.
	v.	*wound, wounded, wounded.* to injure.
	v.	*wind, wound, wound,* to wrap or twist sth around itself or sth else.
Yellow	*adj.*	having colour of lemons or butter.
	adj.	cowardly.
	v.	to become yellow.

2

HOMOPHONES

Abb	*n.*	woof, weft.
Ebb	*n.*	the reflux of tide water in sea.
Abbess	*n.*	nun in charge of a convent.
Abyss	*n.*	very deep hole.
Abbot	*n.*	the head of an abbey.
Abut	*v.*	to lean, to end.
About	*adv.*	approximately.
	prep.	connected with, next to sb/sth.
	adj.	to be close to sth.
Abel	*n.*	the second son of Adam & Eve.
Able	*adj.*	clever or skillful in doing.
	suff.	having the quality of.
Accede	*v.*	to comply with, approve.
Exceed	*v.*	to surpass.
Accept	*v.*	to be agree to receive sth.
Except	*v.*	to leave out, to object.
	prep.	exclusive of.
	conj.	unless.
Access	*n.*	reach.
Axes	*n.*	*plu* of *axis.* lines round a spinning object, earth's axes.
Excess	*n.*	more than is necessary.

Accomplice	*n.*	who helps sb to commit a crime.
Accomplish	*v.*	to succeed in doing sth.
Accord	*v.*	formal agreement.
Occurred	*v.*	happened.
Ach	*excl.*	sorry.
Ache	*v.*	to hurt.
	n.	pain in any part of body.
Adapt	*v.*	to make fit or suitable.
Adept	*adj.*	well skilled.
Add	*v.*	to sum up.
Ad	*abbre.*	advertisement.
Aid	*n.*	assistance sent to help in difficult situation.
	v.	to help, assist.
Aide	*n.*	a person who helps another person.
AIDS	*n.*	*abbre* of Acquired Immune Deficiency.
Ed	*suff.*	having the features of.
Addict	*n.*	a person devoted to a habit of drugs.
Edict	*n.*	order given by a government or king.
Addition	*n.*	act of adding.
Edition	*n.*	the set of copies published at a time.
Adit	*n.*	access, entrance into a mine.
Edit	*v.*	to arrange & prepare for publication.
Advice	*n.*	an opinion or counsel.
Advise	*v.*	to suggest best action to be done.
Advocaat	*n.*	a strong alcoholic drink.
Advocate	*v.*	to support sth publicly.
	n.	lawyer.
Affect	*v.*	to influence.
Effect	*n.*	result.
Affection	*n.*	a gentle feeling of love.
Affectation	*n.*	artificial behaviour designed to impress sb.
Affective	*adj.*	exciting emotion.
Effective	*adj.*	efficient, powerful.

Afterwards	*adv.*	at a later time.
After word	*n.*	a writing at the end of a book.
Age	*n.*	how many years one has lived.
Ages	*n.*	a historical period, very long time.
Age	*v.*	*aged, aged, aging.* process to become older.
	suff.	the action or result of sth, condition or state.
As	*prep.*	to describe quality purpose etc.
	adv.	used to compare.
	conj.	because, although, regarding.
Aggro	*n.*	violent aggressive behaviour.
Agro	*combining form.*	related to farming.
Ail	*v.*	to cause problem.
Aile	*n.*	isle, the side passage in church.
Ale	*n.*	a type of beer.
Alee	*adv.*	towards the wind.
Air	*n.*	mixture of gas that we breathe.
Ear	*n.*	hearing organ.
Heir	*n.*	successor.
Year	*n.*	twelve calendar months.
Aisle	*n.*	the walk way on in a theatre, vehicle etc.
Isle	*n.*	island.
All	*det.*	the whole number of.
	adj. & *pron.*	the whole amount, altogether.
	adv.	completely, totally.
	n.	every thing.
Al	*suff.*	a process or state of.
Awl	*n.*	small tool for boring at sth.
Allay	*v.*	to make less frightened.
Alley	*n.*	a passage.
Ally	*n.*	country supporting another during war.
All ready	*adj.*	completely ready.
Already	*adv.*	before the present time.
A lot, lots	*pron.*	a large amount or number.
Allot	*v.*	to give a share of sth for a purpose.

Aloud	*adv.*	in a loud voice.
Allowed	*v.*	*allow, allowed, allowed.* permitted.
Alow	*adv.*	down below.
Allow	*v.*	to permit.
Altar	*n.*	a platform for offering to God.
Alter	*v.*	to change.
Altogether	*adv.*	completely, in total.
All together	*adj.*	together in one group.
Amen	*interj.*	so be it. used at the end of a prayer.
Omen	*n.*	a sign for future events.
Amend	*v.*	to make better.
Emend	*v.*	to remove faults from.
Anal	*adj.*	of the anus.
Annals	*n.*	historical records of events.
And	*conj.*	also, in addition to, plus.
End	*n.*	last part, aim.
	n.	a person's death.
	v.	to finish.
Angel	*n.*	a spiritual creature.
Angle	*n.*	meeting of two lines.
	v.	to fish with a hook.
	n.	a position from which sth is viewed.
Annex	*v.*	to occupy, to take possession of.
Annexe	*n.*	an addition, a subsidiary building.
Ant	*n.*	a small insect.
Aunt	*n.*	the father's or mother's sister.
Ante	*pref.*	before in time or position.
	n.	player's stake in poker.
Anti	*pref.*	against, opposed to.
Antic	*n.*	a silly trick.
Antique	*adj.*	old.
Appal	*v.*	(also appall). to shake sb very much.
Apple	*n.*	a round fruit.

Apposite	*n.*	appropriate, relevant.
Opposite	*adj.*	facing, contrary, adverse.
Appraise	*v.*	to examine sb to judge him.
Apprise	*v.*	to tell, to warn.
Apprize	*v.*	to evaluate the value or the worth of.
Arc	*n.*	a part of circumference of a circle.
Arch	*adj.*	chief, main.
	combining form.	chief, principal.
	n.	curved part of building.
Ark	*n.*	a large boat, box.
Area	*n.*	region.
Aria	*n.*	melody
Arm	*n.*	part of body
	n.	sleeve.
	n.	wing.
	v.	to make weapons.
Arms	*n.*	weapons.
Alms	*n.*	the items given to poor people.
Arose	*v.*	*arise, arose, arisen.*
Arouse	*v.*	to stimulate, make active, awaken.
Arow	*adv.*	in a row.
Arrow	*n.*	a pointed stick shot from a bow.
Artist	*n.*	a person who creates works of art.
Artiste	*n.*	a professional entertainer.
Ascent	*n.*	act of climbing or moving up.
Assent	*n.*	consent.
Ash tray	*n.*	tray to keep burnt dust, ash etc.
Astray	*v.*	stray out of right path.
Assay	*adv.*	to put to the proof.
Essay	*v.*	to attempt.
	n.	a writing on a particular subject.
At	*prep.*	in, on, towards.
Ate	*v.*	*p.t.* of *eat.*
	suff.	full of or having quality of
Eight	*n*	*& adj.* one more than seven.

Attach	*v.*	to join one thing to another.
Attaché	*n.*	a person who works at an Embassy.
Auger	*n.*	a tool to make holes in wood.
Augur	*v.*	to predict.
Aught	*n.*	anything.
Oat	*n.*	a grain used for food *(jai).*
Ought		*modal verb.* used to express morality & social binding as should is used for duty, obligation & suggestion whereas must is used for compulsion & necessity.
Out	*adv., prep.*	away from the inside.
	n.	a way of avoiding having to do sth.
	v.	to force sb to quit.
	adj.	absent, no longer secret.
	pref.	further, outside, away from.
Owt	*pron.*	anything.
Avail	*v.*	to be of use or value.
Avale	*v.*	to come down.
Aver	*v.*	state to be true.
Ever	*adv.*	at any time, always.
Axe	*n.*	a tool for chopping tree.
Ex	*prep.*	not including sth.
Ex	*pref.*	former.
X	*n.*	a letter of alphabet, meaning 10 in Roman system, symbol used in a stamp in voting, expressing a kiss at the end of a letter, symbol to declare an answer wrong.
Axel	*n.*	shaft on which a wheel runs.
Excel	*v.*	to be superior to.
Aye	*excl.*	yes.
Eye	*n.*	a parts of body to see.
	n.	the hole in the end of a needle.
	n.	hook to fasten clothes.
	v.	to see.

Back	*n.*	the hinder part of the body.
	adj.	located behind.
	v.	support.
Bake	*v.*	to cook by heat.
Beck	*n.*	a small river, stream.
Backer	*n.*	supporter.
Baker	*n.*	bread maker.
Bacon	*n.*	pig's flesh salted & dried.
Beacon	*n.*	a light lit to indicate danger.
Beckon	*v.*	to call.
Bail	*n.*	amount of money paid to the court for release until trial.
	v.	to throw water away from a boat.
Bale	*n.*	misery.
Vale	*n.*	a valley.
Bait	*n.*	food to allure fish.
Bate	*n.*	strife.
Ballet	*n.*	a performance of dancing on stage.
Valet	*n.*	a personal servant.
Wallet	*n.*	a small folding case.
Bam	*excl.*	used to say that sth happens very suddenly.
Balm	*n.*	liquid, cream.
Band	*n.*	a tie, a thin flat strip put around things.
	n.	a group of musicians.
Banned	*v.*	*adj. ban, banned, banned.* prohibited.
Bend	*v.*	*bent, bent.* to curve, to incline.
Wend	*v.*	*wended, wended.* to move or travel slowly somewhere.
Bane	*n.*	curse, ruin.
Bene	*n.*	prayer.
	pref	well
Vain	*adj.*	useless.
Vein	*n.*	a blood vessel.
Ban	*n.*	prohibition, curse.
Ben	*n.*	a mountain peak.

Banish	*v.*	to exile.
Vanish	*v.*	to disappear.
Bard	*n.*	a poet.
Ward	*n.*	a minor under a guardian.
	v.	to protect.
	suff.	towards a direction.
Bare	*adj.*	uncovered.
Bear	*v.*	*bore, borne.* to give birth.
Bear	*v.*	*bore, borne.* to suffer, to support.
Bear	*n.*	a wild animal (*Bhaloo).*
Beer	*n.*	liquor made of malt & hops.
Bere	*n.*	barley.
Bier	*n.*	a frame to carry dead body at funeral.
Byre	*n.*	cowshed.
Bare-ly	*adv.*	rarely.
Barley	*n.*	a plant grown for its grain.
Base	*n.*	foundation, the lowest part of sth.
	adj.	not having moral principles or rules.
Bass	*n.*	lowest pitch in music.
Basis	*n.*	*plu of bases.* the reason for taking an action.
Bash	*n.*	strong fellow.
Vase	*n.*	an ornamental vessel.
Bat	*n.*	cricket bat.
	n.	a winged animal. (*chamgadad*).
Bet	*v.*	to risk money on prediction.
Bait	*n.*	food to allure fish.
Bate	*n.*	strife.
Bawl	*v.*	to shout loudly.
Bowl	*n.*	container.
	v.	to roll ball, to play with bowls.
Bole	*n.*	trunk of a tree.
Boll	*n.*	a seed capsule of cotton.
Bay	*n.*	a gulf.
	adj.	reddish brown.
	v.	to bark as a dog.
Bays	*n.*	honorary garland of victory.
Way	*n.*	road, path.

Be	*pref.*	to make or treat sb/sth.
Be	*v.*	to exist, to become to be present. (is, am, are, was, were, been)
Bee	*n.*	an insect that makes honey.
We	*pron.*	*plu* of 'I'. people in general.
Beach	*n.*	the sandy shore of the sea.
Beech	*n.*	a common forest tree.
Bitch	*n.*	female dog.
Bean	*n.*	seed used as food *(sem)*.
Been	*p.p.*	of the verb *be*.
Beat	*v.*	to thrash.
Beet	*n.*	the red variety vegetable.
Beet	*v.*	to implore.
Beaver	*n.*	an amphibious animal (*udvilau*).
Baver	*n.*	a heavy woolen cloth.
Bedding	*n.*	materials of bed.
Wedding	*n.*	marriage.
Bel	*n.*	measurement of sound equal to 10 decibels.
Bell	*n.*	rung at school, temple etc.
Belie	*v.*	to show to be false.
Belly	*n.*	abdomen.
Belle	*n.*	beautiful woman.
Below	*adv.*	in lower place, under, beneath.
Bellow	*v.*	to roar like a bull.
Bellows	*n.*	instrument to pump a stream of air.
Billow	*n.*	a big wave of the sea.
Willow	*n.*	cricket bats are made of willow tree.
Blow	*n.*	hard stroke.
	v.	*blow, blew, blown.* to move *(wind)*
	v.	to sound horn etc.
Berth	*n.*	a bed in a ship, train etc.
	n.	job.
Birth	*n.*	the act of being born.
Worth	*adj.*	having a value in money etc.
Betel	*n.*	a leaf chewed by Indians *(paan)*
Beetle	*n.*	an insect.
Battle	*n.*	a fight, a struggle.

Bevvy	*n.*	a type of beer.
Bevy	*n.*	a group.
Bivvy	*n.*	temporary shelter.
Bi	*pref.*	meaning twice, double.
By	*prep.*	near, along, during sth.
By	*prep.*	used with doer to show the action performed by, also used after passive verb.
	adv.	past, before long, soon.
	pref.	*(also bye)* less important.
Bye	*n.*	in cricket a run made from a ball going past the wicket.
	interj.	Goodbye.
Buy	*v.*	to purchase.
Bias	*n.*	a turning away from the straight line.
Bice	*n.*	a blue or green pigment.
Bide	*v.*	to dwell permanently.
Vice	*n.*	criminal activities.
		combining form. next in rank to sb who can act on his behalf in his absence.
Vide	*abbre.*	used meaning *'see'* as an instruction writings for more information.
Big	*adj.*	large.
Wig	*n.*	artificial head of hair.
	v.	to scold.
Bile	*n.*	the liquid which the liver produces.
	n.	anger or hatred.
Vile	*adj.*	mean, depraved.
Billed	*v.*	*bill, billed, billed.*
Build	*v.*	to construct.
Bitch	*n.*	a female dog.
	v.	to make unkind & critical remarks about sb.
Which	*pron., det.*	to ask for or refer to.
Witch	*n.*	a woman who is believed to have magic powers.
Bite	*v.*	*bit, bitten.* to cut.
Bight	*n.*	a bend in shore.
Byte	*n.*	a unit of information stored in a computer.

Blanch	*v.*	to become white or pale.
Blench	*v.*	shy away, as in fear.
Bland	*adj.*	dull & uninteresting.
Blend	*v.*	mix or mingle, look good together.
	n.	mixture.
Blew	*v.*	*blow, blew, blown.*
Blue	*n.*	sky colour.
Bloat	*v.*	to cause to swell.
Blot	*v.*	to stain.
Block	*n.*	two or more countries combined.
Block	*n.*	obstacle.
	v.	to stop sth to flow.
Bloke	*n.*	*(informal)* man.
Boar	*n.*	a wild pig.
Bore	*v.*	*bear, bore, borne.*
Bore	*n.*	an uninteresting person.
Bore	*v.*	make a hole with a drill.
	v.	make sb feel weary & bored.
	n.	high wave caused by tide.
Board	*n.*	a piece of wood etc.
	n.	group of people.
	n.	meals provided in a hotel etc.
	v.	get on plane, ship.
Bored	*adj.*	uninteresting.
Boarder	*n.*	one who lives in a hostel.
Border	*n.*	edge, margin, frontier.
Boggy	*adj.*	marshy.
Bogie	*n.*	a long carriage of a train.
Bold	*adj.*	courageous.
Bowled	*v.*	*bowl, bowled, bowled.*
Bole	*n.*	trunk of tree.
Boll	*n.*	seed containing part of cotton plant..
Bowl	*n.*	round container with an open top.
Bowl	*n.*	large heavy ball.

Bomb	*n.*	an explosive shell.
Womb	*n.*	the female organ where baby develops before birth.
Bon	*adj.*	good.
Bone	*n.*	the hard parts inside the body.
Bonne	*n.*	a maid servant.
Bootee		(also bootie).
	n.	a baby's sock also used as shoes.
Booty	*n.*	loot.
Born	*v.*	*p.p.* of *bear.* brought forth.
	adj.	natural.
Borne	*v.*	*p.p.* of *bear.* carried, supported, to stand.
Borne	*adj.*	carried by.
Borrow	*v.*	to take & use sth from sb & then return it.
Borough	*n.*	a division of a big town.
Burrow	*n.*	dig, hole or tunnel.
Bosh	*n.*	nonsense.
Boss	*n.*	a person who is in charge of sth & the other follow him.
Bote	*n.*	compensation.
Boat	*n.*	a wooden structure to row in the water.
Vote	*n.*	when we express our opinion or choice in any election.
Bough	*n.*	the branch of a tree.
Bow	*n.*	by which we shoot arrows.
	v.	to bend as a sign of respect.
Vow	*n.*	a solemn promise, an oath.
Bowel	*n.*	the entrails.
	v.	to pass solid waste out of the body.
Vowel	*n.*	*a, e, i, o, u.* in English alphabet.
Brake	*n.*	a place over grown with wild plants, hedges etc..
	n.	a block to stop.
Break	*v.*	*broke, broken..* to shatter.
Brawn	*n.*	physical strength.
Brown	*n.*	chocolate colour.

Breach	*v.*	to break.
Breech	*n.*	the back or lower part of sth.
Bread	*n.*	baked food made of flour.
Braid	*n.*	plait of hair.
Breed	*v.*	to beget.
	v.	a certain class of animals.
Bred	*v.*	*p.t. & p.p.* of *breed.*
Brews	*v.*	to make beer.
Bridal	*adj.*	belonging to a bride.
Bridle	*n.*	a leather strip to control horse.
Bruise	*n.*	mark on skin after being hit.
Bro	*n.*	a brother.
Brow	*n.*	forehead.
Burro	*n.*	a small donkey.
Broach	*v.*	to raise a subject for discussion.
Brooch	*n.*	a piece of jewellery.
Burk	*v.*	to suppress.
Burke	*v.*	to murder.
Burley	*n.*	a kind of fine light tobacco.
Burly	*adj.*	of stout build.
Burst	*n.*	a short period of a particular activity.
	v.	break into pieces.
Bursty	*adj.*	used to describe data sent in signals.
Bust	*n.*	a statue of upper front part of body.
Bus	*n.*	a large road vehicle that carries passengers.
Bush	*n.*	cluster of shrubs.
Buss	*n.*	a kiss.
But	*conj.*	however, yet.
	prep.	except.
	adv.	only.
	n.	a given reason for not doing sth.
Butt	*n.*	thick end of a weapon, a container *esp* for liquids, bits of smoked cigarette.
	v.	to hit or push hard with head.
Butte	*n.*	a hill that is flat on top.

Cabble	*v.*	to smash into fragments.
Cable	*n.*	a thick strong rope.
Cache	*n.*	a hidden store of weapons.
Catch	*v.*	to seize & hold, capture.
Cadge	*v.*	to beg.
Cage	*n.*	a place of confinement.
	v.	to imprison.
Cad	*n.*	a vulgar fellow.
Cade	*adj.*	tame.
Cain	*n.*	any murderer.
Can	*n.*	a container.
	v.	fire, sack.
	v.	*modal verb,* be able. *(used to convey ability, strength, power, skill, permission, nature etc.)*
Cane	*n.*	an easily bent stick.
Call	*v.*	to speak loudly.
Caul	*n.*	a membrane covering the head of a child at birth.
Coll	*v.*	to embrace.
Cam	*n.*	the part of machine for changing its movement.
	n.	a feeling of friendship & trust among people.
Calm	*adj.*	not excited, quiet.
	v.	to make quiet & more relaxed.
Candid	*adj.*	frank, fair.
Candied	*adj.*	sweet.
Cannon	*n.*	a large gun.
Canon	*n.*	church decree.
Cant	*n.*	insincere talk.
Can't	*auxi.*	short form of *can not.*
Canvas	*n.*	rough, strong cloth.
Canvass	*v.*	to go & ask for votes.
Cap	*n.*	a brimless hat.
Cape	*n.*	land touching the ea.
	n.	a cloak.

Carat	*n.*	a unit for measuring the weights of precious stones.
Carrot	*n.*	a root vegetable.
	n.	incentive.
Career	*n.*	profession.
Carrier	*n.*	one who or which carries sth.
Caries	*n.*	decay in teeth or bone.
Carries	*v.*	*carry, carries.*
Carpal	*n.*	a bone of the wrist.
Carpel	*n.*	part of leaf.
Cast	*n.*	mould, a throw
	v.	to look, to throw.
	v.	to shed.
Caste	*n.*	any class of the society.
Caw	*n.*	*& v.* the sound made by crow.
Cow	*n.*	the female ox.
	v.	to subdue by threats.
Cede	*v.*	to give up.
Seed	*n.*	sow seeds to grow plants.
Ceil	*v.*	to cover the inner roof of room.
Seal	*n.*	sea animal.
	v.	to mark with seal.
Ceiling	*n.*	the inside roof of a room.
	n.	top limit.
Sealing	*n.*	act of affixing a seal.
	v.	to close.
Cell	*n.*	a small room.
	n.	plant cell.
	n.	electric battery.
Sell	*v.*	to give in exchange of money.
Shall	*modal verb.*	used with first person in simple future & with second & third persons to express threat, promise, determination etc.
Shell	*n.*	a hard outer covering.
	v.	to strip off the shell.

Cellar	*n.*	a room below the ground.
Sailor	*n.*	a seaman, a mariner.
Seller	*n.*	one who sells.
Cense	*v.*	to perfume with incense.
Sense	*n.*	ability to perceive.
Censor	*n.*	an officer to examine books etc.
Censer	*n.*	container for burning incense.
Censure	*n.*	blame.
Sensor	*n.*	a device that can react to light, heat etc.
Cereal	*adj.*	pertaining to edible grains.
Serial	*adj.*	of or in a series.
	n.	a television or radio serial.
Cession	*n.*	act of surrendering.
Session	*n.*	term.
Chafe	*v.*	to make hot by rubbing.
Chaff	*n.*	the covering separated from grain.
Chap	*n.*	a young fellow.
Chape	*n.*	the plate of metal at the point of.
Chef	*n.*	head cook.
Chary	*adj.*	cautious, shy, unwilling.
Charry	*adj.*	like charcoal.
Cherry	*n.*	a kind of small tree.
Chauffer	*n.*	a small portable furnace.
Chauffeur	*n.*	the driver of a car.
Cheap	*adj.*	of the little value.
Cheep	*v.*	to chirp.
Chief	*n.*	a leader.
Chip	*n.*	a small piece of wood metal etc.
Cheat	*v.*	to deceive.
	n.	a dishonest person.
Chit	*n.*	a short letter or note.
Check	*n.*	stop.
	v.	to examine sth.
Cheque	*n.*	an order to pay money.
Cheer	*n.*	good spirits.
Chair	*n.*	a single seat with a back.

Chest	*n.*	a strong box.
	n.	the breast.
Chaste	*adj.*	pure, virtuous.
Chilli	*n.*	small green or red fruit used in cooking.
Chilly	*adj.*	too cold to be comfortable.
Cite	*v.*	to refer to, quote.
Site	*n.*	situation.
Sight	*n.*	spectacle, aim, thing seen.
Clarence	*n.*	a four wheeled carriage.
Clearance	*n.*	the act of clearing, net profit.
Clause	*n.*	*(grammar)* a part of sentence that has a subject & predicate.
Claws	*n.*	nails of animals or birds.
Close	*v.*	shut, end.
	adj.	near in space or time, almost, likely.
	adv.	not far away.
Cloak	*n.*	a loose upper garment.
Clock	*n.*	an instrument to show time.
Clour	*n.*	a knock.
Colour	*n.*	hue.
Collage	*n.*	collection of things.
College	*n.*	educational institution.
Collide	*v.*	to come into conflict.
Collied	*adj.*	sooty.
Colonel	*n.*	an army officer.
Colonial	*adj.*	pertaining to colony.
Coma	*n.*	very deep sleep, the head of a tree.
Comma	*n.*	punctuation mark (,) used to mark a shortest pause.
Come	*v.*	to move to or toward sb.
Cum	*prep.*	*(used for linking two nouns).* and, as well as.
Compare	*v.*	to examine the similarity or difference between two objects.
Compere	*n.*	a person who introduces the people in a
	n.	programme.
Compeer	*n.*	an equal, an associate.

Complement	*n.*	sth that makes up a whole.
	v.	to complete.
	adj.	together making up whole.
Compliment	*n.*	praise & admiration of sb.
Con	*v.*	to study carefully.
Cone	*n.*	a solid body tapering to point from a circular base.
Concent	*n.*	harmony of sounds.
Consent	*v.*	to allow.
	n.	agreement.
Concur	*v.*	to agree.
Conquer	*v.*	to win.
Conker	*n.*	small shiny brown nut of horse chestnut tree.
Confidant	*n.*	a person to whom one confides.
Confident	*adj.*	bold, self reliant.
Contend	*v.*	to compete
Content	*n.*	the things contained.
	n.	contentment.
Content	*adj.*	happy & satisfied.
	v.	to accept & be satisfied.
Contained	*v.*	*p.t.* & *p.p.* of *contain.*
Cop	*v.*	to catch or arrest.
	n.	a police man.
Cope	*v.*	to deal successfully with a difficulty.
Coup	*n.*	a stroke or blow.
	n.	a stroke or blow.
Coup (also coup d'etat)	*n.*	a sudden & illegal change of government.
Coupe	*n.*	a type of car.
Coral	*n.*	a substance found in the sea.
Corral	*n.*	an enclosure for cattle.
Corps	*n.*	a branch of the army, a body of people, troops.
Corpse	*n.*	a dead body.
Costal	*adj.*	pertaining to the ribs or the side of the body.
Coastal	*adj.*	pertaining to the coast.
Councillor	*n.*	a member of a council.
Counsellor	*n.*	an adviser.

Cousin	*n.*	the son or daughter of uncle.
Cosine	*n.*	ratio of the length of the side next to an acute angle.
Cuisine	*n.*	way of cooking.
Crack	*v.*	to break.
	n.	a narrow opening to peep or sth to come out.
	adj.	expert.
Creak	*v.*	to squeak.
Creek	*n.*	small stream.
Craw	*n.*	the crop of a bird or animal.
Crow	*n.*	a black bird.
	v.	to boast.
Create	*v.*	to make sth happen or exist.
Crate	*n.*	a large wooden container.
Critic	*n.*	one who discusses & judges any kind of artistic work.
Critique	*n.*	a critical essay or review.
Crop	*n.*	harvest.
	n.	a part of bird's throat.
	n.	a short whip used by horse riders.
	v.	to cut short.
Croup	*n.*	disease during cough in children.
Cue	*n.*	a signal for action.
	n.	a long stick used in Billiards, Pool & Snooker.
Queue	*n.*	a line of vehicles or people.
Currant	*n.*	a small raisin without seed.
Current	*adj.*	of the present.
Cygnet	*n.*	a young swan.
Signet	*n.*	*(ring)* with design cut into it.
	n.	a stream.
Daily	*adj.*	happening everyday.
	n.	daily newspaper.
Dally	*v.*	to waste time.
Dairy	*n.*	where milk is sold.
Diary	*n.*	a book of daily record of events.

Dais	*n.*	the raised platform.
Dice	*n.*	a small six sided piece used in games.
Days	*n.*	*plu* of day.
Daze	*n.*	confused state.
Dam	*n.*	a barrier stopping water.
Dame	*n.*	a mistress.
Dam	*n.*	a barrier stopping water.
Damn	*v.*	to condemn.
	adj.	annoyed.
	v.	to show anger
	n.	to not care about.
Dammed	*adj.*	held or kept back.
Damned	*adj.*	condemned, cursed.
Dare	*v.*	to venture.
Deer	*n.*	a wild animal.
Dear	*adj.*	beloved.
	adv.	at a high price.
	n.	a kind person.
Dire	*adj.*	terrible, dreadful.
Daunt	*v.*	to discourage, to frighten.
Don't	*v.*	do not.
Dawn	*n.*	day break, a new beginning.
Down	*adj.*	*& prep.* downward direction.
	adv.	at a lower level.
	prep.	along to.
	v.	to finish a drink or eat sth quickly.
	adj.	sad or depressed.
	n.	fine soft feathers of bird.
Don	*n.*	a teacher at a university.
	v.	to put clothes etc.
Done	*adj.*	finished, completed.
	excl.	to show agreed.
	v.	*do, did, done.*
Debt	*n.*	sum of money that sb owes.
Debit	*n.*	sum of money deducted from a bank account.
Det	*abbre.*	detective, determiner.

Deaf	*adj.*	unable to hear.
Def	*adj.*	excellent.
Dearie	*n.*	used to address in a friendly way.
Dreary	*adj.*	dull.
Decent	*adj.*	becoming, modest.
Descent	*n.*	ancestary.
	n.	downward slope.
Dissent	*v.*	to differ in opinion.
Deep	*adj.*	going down.
Dip	*v.*	to take a dip in water, let down in a liquid.
Defer	*v.*	to postpone.
Differ	*v.*	to disagree.
Deference	*n.*	regard, respect.
Difference	*n.*	unlikeness, disagreement.
De-file	*v.*	to make dirty.
	n.	a narrow way through mountains.
Defuse	*v.*	to make a situation less tense.
Diffuse	*v.*	to spread.
	adj.	not clear or easy to understand.
Defy	*v.*	to challenge.
Deify	*v.*	to make Godlike, to worship
Deity	*n.*	a god or goddess worshipped in a religious place.
Ditty	*n.*	a simple song.
Depositary	*n.*	trustworthy.
Depository	*n.*	store house.
Desert	*n.*	a desolate place.
	v.	to leave, to abandon.
	adj.	barren.
Deserts	*n.*	good or bad qualities.
Dessert	*n.*	sweet food served at the end of a meal.
Dissert	*v.*	to discourse.
Dew	*n.*	small frozen drops of water.
Duo	*n.*	two people performing together.
Due	*adj.*	owing, fit, claimable.

	adv.	exactly, in a straight line.
	n.	a thing that should be given to sb as a right.
Due to	*adj.*	caused by sth, because of sb/sth.

Die	*n.*	*plu* of dice used in game of chess or dice *(pasa).*
	n.	*plu* of dies. a metal block used for stamping.
	v.	to expire.
Dye	*n.*	a colouring substance.

Dingey, Dinghy	*n.*	a small open boat.
Dingy	*adj.*	dirty coloured.

Discreet	*adj.*	tactful.
Discrete	*adj.*	separate.

Discus	*n.*	a circular piece of metal thrown at athletic contest.
Discuss	*v.*	to talk about.

Does	*n.*	female deer.
	v.	do, does.
Doughs	*n.*	unbaked loaves of bread.
Doze	*v.*	to sleep.

Dollar	*n.*	the monetary unit of USA & Canada.
Dolour	*n.*	sorrow, woe.

Dolman	*n.*	long loose garment.
Dolmen	*n.*	old monument.

Door	*n.*	a flat object to open or lock the room.
Doer	*n.*	a person who does things.
Dor	*n.*	a beetle.

Dory	*n.*	a flat bottomed boat.
Dowry	*n.*	money or property given to groom by bride's parents.

Dose	*n.*	a portion.
Doze	*v.*	to sleep lightly.
Dodge	*n.*	a clever & dishonest trick.
	v.	to avoid doing sth.

Dosh	*n.*	money.
Doss	*v.*	to sleep somewhere.

Dote	*v.*	to feel & show great love for sb.
Dot	*n.*	small round mark (...) used as punctuation marks.

Dual	*adj.*	of two.
Duel	*n.*	a fight or contest between two persons.
Dwell	*v.*	*dwelt, dwelt.* to inhabit
Each	*pron.*	every .
Etch	*v.*	to cut a pattern.
Itch	*n.*	uncomfortable feeling on skin.
Eagar	*adj.*	anxious.
Eagre	*n.*	high tidal wave at river mouth.
Ear	*n.*	spike or head of a corn.
	n.	the organ of hearing.
Air	*n.*	the substance which we breathe.
Airs	*n.*	show of pride & vanity.
Heir	*n.*	successor.
Year	*n.*	twelve months make a year.
Early	*adj.*	before the usual time.
Yearly	*adj.*	once a year or every year.
Earn	*v.*	to get money for the work done.
Yearn	*v.*	to long.
Urn	*n.*	a vase for holding the ashes of the dead.
Eat	*v.*	to put food into the mouth & chew.
It	*pron.*	things named or in question.
Eave	*n.*	the lower edge of roof.
Eve	*n.*	time just before an important event.
Echo	*n.*	reverberation.
Eco	*combining form.*	connected with the environment.
Eco	*abbre.*	ecology, economics.
Eek	*excl.*	used to express fear or surprise.
Eke	*v.*	to increase gradually.
Elicit	*v.*	to draw out, to extract.
Illicit	*adj.*	prohibited, unlawful, improper.
Eligible	*adj.*	fit to be chosen, suitable.
Illegible	*adj.*	unreadable.
Elusive	*adj.*	difficult to describe.
Illusive	*adj.*	deceptive.
Embail	*v.*	to encircle.
Embale	*v.*	to make up as into a bundle.

Emerge	*v.*	to appear.
Immerge	*v.*	to drop in liquid.
Eminent	*adj.*	sb or sth that stands in some way.
Imminent	*adj.*	just about to happen.
Immanent	*adj.*	present every where.
Emperil	*v.*	to put in danger.
Imperil	*v.*	to endanger.
Empire	*n.*	kingdom of a ruler.
Umpire	*n.*	referee of a game.
Empress	*n.*	the wife of an emperor.
Impress	*n.*	a stamp, a seal.
	v.	to influence.
En	*pref.*	in the sense of in or into.
In	*prep, adj.*	within an area or space, inside, within a period of time.
	pref.	the opposite of.
Inn	*n.*	a public house providing food & lodging for travellers.
Enate	*adj.*	growing out.
Innate	*adj.*	inborn, natural, inherent.
Endanger	*v.*	to put a harmful situation.
In danger	*adj.*	likely to face unpleasant happening.
Endo	*pref.*	within.
Endow	*v.*	to give a dowry, to furnish with.
Enfant	*n.*	a child.
Infant	*n.*	baby, minor.
Enteritis	*n.*	inflammation of intestines.
Interstice	*n.*	a chink, a gap.
Envelop	*v.*	to cover, to hide.
Envelope	*n.*	the cover of a letter.
Ere	*adv & conj.*	before, sooner than.
	excl.	denoting the action done next.

ER	*abbre.*	Emergency Room.
Era	*n.*	epoch.
Err	*v.*	to commit a mistake.
Erupt	*v.*	break out forcibly or suddenly.
Irrupt	*v.*	break into forcibly or suddenly.
Eruption	*n.*	explosion.
Irruption	*n.*	sudden invasion.
Escape	*v.*	to slip away, to avoid.
Scape	*v.*	to escape.
	n.	an invasion.
	n.	leafless flower stalk.
	combining form.	a view or scene of.
Especially	*adv.*	particularly.
Specially	*adv.*	for a particular purpose.
Espouse	*v.*	to give support to a belief, policy etc.
	v.	to marry, to adopt.
Spouse	*n.*	a husband or wife.
Espy	*v.*	to catch sight of spy.
Spy	*n.*	detective.
Esquire	*n.*	one of two attendants on a knight.
Squire	*n.*	a subordinate in rank to a knight.
Expanse	*n.*	a wide & open area of sth.
Expense	*n.*	the money spent on sth.
Expansive	*adj.*	covering a large amount of space.
	adj.	friendly & willing to talk.
Expensive	*adj.*	costly.
Extant	*adj.*	still standing or existing.
Extent	*n.*	how large, important, etc. sth is.
Eye	*n.*	the organ to see.
	v.	to see.
I	*pron.*	first person *singular.*
Fad	*n.*	hobby, craze.
Fade	*v.*	to wither.

Fain	*adv.*	gladly.
Fan	*n.*	an device to produce currents of air.
Fan	*n.*	some one who likes & admires a famous person or sth.
Feign	*v.*	to invent, to pretend.
Feign	*v.*	to give a false appearance.
Fen	*n.*	a low lying flat marshy land.
Faint	*adj.*	dim or weak.
	v.	to swoon.
Feint	*n.*	pretence, attack or blow.
Fair	*adj.*	clear, free from fault, beautiful.
	n.	a large public event.
Fare	*n.*	the sum paid by passenger on vehicle.
Fear	*n.*	dread.
Fairy	*n.*	a small creature with wings & magic power.
Faerie		(also faery).
	n.	fairy land.
Ferry	*v.*	to row boat.
Fiery	*adj.*	consisting fire, irritable.
Faun	*n.*	Roman God of farmers.
Fawn	*n.*	a young deer.
	v.	to show affection.
Fay	*n.*	fairy.
Fey	*adj.*	fated to die soon, sensitive.
Feat	*n.*	an action that needs skill or courage.
Feet	*n.*	*plu* of *foot.*
Fit	*v.*	to be suitable.
	v.	to agree.
	adj.	healthy & strong.
	n.	convulsion, bout.
	n.	match.
Feel	*v.*	perceive, to know by touch.
	v.	be aware.
	n.	impression created.
Feal	*adj.*	faithful.
Fill	*v.*	to make full.
	n.	a full supply.
	n.	as much willing to accept.

Fever	*n.*	an illness of high temperature.
Favour	*n.*	a gracious act, approval, goodwill.
Fiancé	*n.*	the man that a woman is engaged to.
Fiancée	*n.*	the woman that a man is engaged to.
File	*n.*	container for papers etc.
	n.	a collection of information on computer.
	n.	a metal tool for cutting.
	v.	to put & keep documents.
Phial	*n.*	small bottle for medicine etc.
Find	*v.*	to discover.
Fined	*adj.*	charged a penalty.
Fir	*n.*	an evergreen tree with needle like leaves.
Fur	*n.*	the short fine soft hair of certain animals.
Flake	*n.*	light fleecy particle.
Fleck	*n.*	a speck or streak.
Floe	*n.*	a large sheet of floating ice.
Flaw	*n.*	defect, fault.
Flow	*v.*	to move steadily in one direction.
	n.	continuous talk by sb.
Flea	*n.*	a very small jumping insect without wings.
Flee	*v.*	*flee, fled, fled.* to run away very quickly.
Flew	*v.*	*p.t.* of *fly.*
Flu	*n.*	an infectious disease like bad cold.
Flue	*n.*	a pipe that takes smoke.
Flip	*n.*	flick.
	v.	somersault.
Fillip	*v.*	to incite, boost.
Phillips	*adj.*	*(of a screw or screw driver)* with a cross shaped part for cutting.
Foggy	*adj.*	full of fog.
Fogey, fogy	*n.*	old fashioned person.
Fool	*n.*	idiot, jester.
Full	*adj.*	with no empty space, complete, busy.
	adv.	completely.
	v.	to cleanse & thicken cloth in mill.

Ful	*suff.*	full of, having the quality of.
Fuel	*n.*	burning material.
Foul	*adj.*	dirty, obscene, wicked.
Forbear	*v.*	to refrain.
Forebear	*n.*	an ancestor.
Forgo	*v.*	to abstain from, to renounce.
Forego	*v.*	to precede.
Foreword	*n.*	an introductory note to a book.
Forward	*adv.*	towards a place in front, in a progressive way.
	adj.	perverse.
Fort	*n.*	a fortified place.
Forte		one's strong point.
Forth	*adv.*	towards, out or away.
Fourth	*adj.*	number four in series.
	n.	a quarter.
Foul	*adj.*	dirty & smelling bad, offensive.
	n.	an act in the game that is against the rules.
Fowl	*n.*	a bird kept for meat, eggs.
Freeze	*v.*	to turn to ice.
Frieze	*n.*	a decoration along a wall.
Fridge	*n.*	refrigerator.
Frizz	*v.*	to curl, to crisp.
Freight	*n.*	hire of a ship.
Fret	*v.*	to wear away by friction.
	n.	irritation.
Fret	*n.*	crossbar on fingerboard of a guitar.
Fright	*n.*	sudden fear.
Fume	*v.*	to be angry about sth.
Fumes	*n.*	smoke, gas etc.
Funeral	*n.*	the burial ceremony.
Funereal	*adj.*	mournful, dismal.
Furry	*adj.*	covered with fur.
Fury	*n.*	extreme anger, rage.

Gabble	*v.*	to speak quickly.
Gable	*n.*	the triangular part of a wall.
Gage	*n.*	a pledge.
Gauge	*n.*	a device to measure the amount or level.
	n.	the distance between the railway line.
Gauze	*n.*	a thin transparent fabric.
Gaze	*v.*	to stare.
Gait	*n.*	manner of walking or running.
Gate	*n.*	an entrance.
Get	*v.*	to obtain, to catch, to reach.
Genteel	*adj.*	polite, elegant, well-bred.
Gentle	*adj.*	mild, placid, meek, tender, docile.
Gig	*n.*	rowing boat for racing.
Jig	*n.*	quick dance.
Gild	*v.*	to cover with gold.
Guild	*n.*	an organization or club.
Gin	*n.*	a machine for separating seeds from cotton.
Jinn	*n.*	spirits.
Glair	*n.*	white of egg.
Glare	*n.*	an intense light.
Globe	*n.*	a ball shaped world map.
Glove	*n.*	a hand covering.
Grantee	*n.*	a person to whom a grant is made.
Guarantee	*n.*	security, an assurance, a pledge.
Greed	*n.*	an eager desire, avarice.
Grid	*n.*	a frame of bars.
Green	*adj.*	grass coloured.
Greens	*n.*	*plu.* vegetables.
Grin	*v.*	to smile broadly.
Groan	*n.*	low sound expressing displeasure.
Grown	*v.*	*grow, grew, grown.*
Hand made	*adj.*	made by hand.
Hand maid	*n.*	female servant.

Haven	*n.*	a harbour, a refuse.
Heaven	*n.*	sky, God's abode.
Haw	*adv.*	hum.
How	*adv.*	in what way or manner, however.
Hay	*n.*	dry grass used food for animals.
Hey	*excl.*	shout.
Hoarse	*adj.*	rough voice.
Horse	*n.*	an animal.
Ideal	*adj.*	perfect, imaginary.
Idle	*adj.*	inactive, lazy.
Idol	*n.*	an image that is worshipped.
Idyl, Idyll	*n.*	a short pastoral poem.
Idem	*adv.*	from the same book, article, etc.
Idiom	*n.*	group of words whose meaning is different from the meanings of the individual words.
Ill	*adj.*	sick.
	adv.	badly or in an unpleasant way.
	n.	a problem or harmful thing.
I'll	*short form* I will.	
Inapt	*adj.*	inappropriate.
Inept	*adj.*	unskillful, unsuitable.
In fact	*n.*	in reality.
Infect	*v.*	to communicate disease by contact.
Inter	*v.*	to bury a dead person.
	pref.	between, from one to another.
Enter	*v.*	to come or go into sth.
	v.	to join institution.
Jail	*n., v.*	*(also gaol)* prison, imprison.
Jell	*v.*	gel.
Jealous	*adj.*	envious.
Zealous	*adj.*	having energy and enthusiasm.
Jink	*n.*	quick illusory turn.
Zinc	*n.*	a white metal.
Juggler	*n.*	an entertainer.
Jugular	*n.*	veins on either side of the neck.

Jumble	*n.*	a thin sweet cake.
Jumbel	*v.*	to mix or move about confusedly.
Kennel	*n.*	a place for dog.
Kernel	*n.*	whole grain of cereal.
Kettle	*n.*	a vessel for boiling water.
Cattle	*n.*	domestic livestock.
Knap	*n.*	the summit of a hill.
Nap	*n.*	a short sleep.
Nape	*n.*	the back of the neck.
Knave	*n.*	a clever trickster.
	n.	a playing card depicting jokester.
Nave	*n.*	the central interior of church.
Knickers	*n.*	short pants.
Nickers	*n.*	neighing of horse.
Knight	*n.*	a champion in war.
Night	*n.*	*opp* of *day.*
Knit	*v.*	to weave into a network.
Nit	*n.*	the egg of louse.
Neat	*adj.*	tidy.
	n.	ox, cow or bull.
Knock	*v.*	to strike with something hard.
Nock	*v.*	to adjust arrow to bow string.
Know	*v.*	to be aware of.
No	*adj.*	none.
Label	*n.*	tag, ticket.
Level	*n.*	a particular standard or quality.
	adj.	flat, equal.
	v.	to raze.
Libel	*n.*	printing a false statement about sb.
Lac	*n.*	lakh.
	n.	a resinous substance.
Lack	*n.*	want, deficiency.
Lake	*n.*	a large stench of water.
Lace	*n.*	a string for fastening *(shoes etc).*
Lash	*n.*	eyelash, sharp blow with a whip.

	v.	fasten or bind tightly with cord etc.
Lash	*v.*	to strike with a whip.
Lass	*n.*	a girl.

Lad	*n.*	a boy.
Lade	*v.*	to load, to burden.
Laid	*adj.*	put down.
Laid	*v.*	*lay, laid, laid*

Laddie	*n.*	a boy.
Lady	*n.*	woman.

Lag	*v.*	to move slowly, to fall behind.
Leg	*n.*	a limb.

Lain	*v.*	*lie, lay, lain.*
Lane	*n.*	a narrow street or road.

Lame	*adj.*	crippled.
	n.	a type of cloth with gold or silver thread.
Lamb	*n.*	a young sheep.
	n.	an innocent person.

Lass	*n.*	*(also lassie)* a girl, a young woman.
Less	*det.*	a smaller amount of.
	adv.	not so much.
	prep.	minus.
	suff.	without.
Lessee	*n.*	a person who takes on lease.

Late	*adj.*	near the end of a period of time.
	adv.	after the expected, arranged or usual time.
Let	*v.*	to give sb permission to do sth.
	v.	to allow sb to use a room etc. in return of payment.
	aux.	to permit, to allow.
	v.	to lease.
	n.	impediment, prohibition.
	suff.	used in sense of small.

Later	*adj.*	subsequent.
Latter	*adj.*	*opp* of former.
Letter	*n.*	small or capital letter of alphabet.
	n.	written message addressed to sb.

Lavatory	*n.*	a place for washing, urinal.
Laboratory	*n.*	a place for scientific experiments.
Law	*n.*	a rule or ordinance established by authority.
Low	*adj.*	not high, not bright.
	adv.	near the bottom of sth.
	n.	a low figure
	v.	a sound of cow, moo.
Lo	*interj.*	look, behold.
	excl.	used to say when surprised.
Loo	*n.*	a toilet/bathroom.
Lay	*n.*	a narrative poem, song.
	v.	*p.t.* of lie. *lie, lay, lain.* to place.
	adj.	unprofessional.
	v.	*laid, laid.* to set, to lay eggs.
	n.	a partner in sex.
Ley	*n.*	an imaginary line, grass land.
Ly	*suff.*	in the said manner.
Lead	*n.*	a grey metal.
Lead	*v.*	to guide, to conduct.
Led	*v.*	*p.t & p.p.* of *lead.*
Leak	*n.*	water letting out.
Leek	*n.*	a plant having bulbs.
Lick	*v.*	to take by drawing the tongue.
Leap	*v.*	to spring up.
	n.	a jump.
Least	*det, adj.*	smallest. *(less, lesser, least).*
Lest	*conj.*	for fear that, in case.
Lip	*n.*	parts of mouth.
List	*n.*	a catalogue, the edge of cloth.
	v.	to enlist.
	v.	to desire, to listen, lean.
Ledger	*n.*	a book to write accounts.
Leisure	*n.*	spare time.
Leman	*n.*	a lover or mistress.
Lemon	*n.*	an acid fruit of orange family.
Lessen	*v.*	to decrease, to make less.
Lesson	*n.*	a topic taught, a punishment.
Listen	*v.*	to hear.

Levee	*n.*	a reception.
	n.	an embankment.
Levy	*v.*	to impose, to raise.
	n.	tax paid to government.
Lever	*n.*	a device to operate a machinery.
Leaver	*n.*	a person who is away from duty with permission of competent authority.
Liver	*n.*	an organ of body.
Lie	*n.*	untruth.
	v.	*lie, lied, lied.* to tell a lie, to deceive.
	v.	*lie, lay, lain.* to take rest.
Lye	*n.*	an alkaline solution.
Ly	*suff.*	in the said manner.
Lief	*adv.*	gladly.
Leaf	*n.*	a green part of a tree.
Light	*n.*	a lamp.
	adj.	bright.
	adj.	not heavy.
Lite	*adj.*	having few calories of food.
Lightening	*v.*	lessening.
Lightning	*n.*	an electric flash in the sky.
Lighting	*n.*	provision of light in a place.
Litre	*n.*	(also liter). measure of liquid.
Littre	*n.*	a hand carriage to carry the dead or injured.
Litter	*n.*	rubbish.
Load	*n.*	a burden.
Lode	*n.*	metal in the ground or in rocks.
Loaf	*n.*	a separate piece of bread.
	v.	to hang about/around.
Laugh	*v.*	to express happiness by sound movement.
Lough	*n.*	a lake.
Loath, loth	*adj.*	unwilling, reluctant.
Loathe	*v.*	to detest, to abominate.
Loin	*n.*	the part above the hips.
Lion	*n.*	a wild animal known as king of forest.

Lone	*adj.*	solitary.
Lawn	*n.*	yard or park.
Loan	*n.*	money or object lent.
Look Over	*n.*	to look to examine quickly.
Over Look	*n.*	fail to notice.
Loot	*v.*	to steal things.
	n.	booty.
Lute	*n.*	a musical instrument played like a guitar.
Lop	*v.*	to chop.
Lope	*v.*	to run with long steps.
Lumber	*n.*	lower back.
Lumber	*n.*	piece of junk or timber.
Mad	*adj.*	insane.
Made	*v.*	*p.t. & p.p.* of *make.*
Maid	*n.*	unmarried woman, a girl servant.
Madden	*v.*	to become mad.
Maiden	*n.*	a girl.
	adj.	unmarried or virgin.
Madam	*n.*	a polite term of address to a lady.
Madame	*n.*	a married woman.
Magnate	*n.*	a rich & powerful person.
Magnet	*n.*	metal that attracts iron.
Mail	*n.*	letters & parcels sent by post.
	v.	to cloth an armour, to post.
Mal	*pref.*	denoting bad.
Maize	*n.*	Indian corn.
Maze	*n.*	a labyrinth.
Male	*n.*	*opp.* of *female.*
Main	*adj.*	principal, chief.
Mane	*n.*	the long hair on the neck of a horse or lion.
Manes	*n.*	souls of ancestors.
Man	*n.*	an adult male human.
Men	*n.*	*plu* of *man.*

Malady	*n.*	sickness.
Melody	*n.*	sweet sound, a tune.
Manager	*n.*	one who manages.
Manger	*n.*	an arrangement or trough in which animals eat food.
Manor	*n.*	a landed estate.
Manure	*n.*	animal excrement.
Miner	*n.*	worker in mines.
Minor	*n.*	a person under 18.
Mantle	*n.*	a cloak, a covering.
Mental	*adj.*	related to or of the mind.
Marble	*n.*	white stone.
Marvel	*n.*	wonderful thing.
Mare	*n.*	a female horse.
Mayor	*n.*	the head of the municipality.
Mere	*n.*	a pond or lake.
	adj.	only this and nothing else.
Mark	*v.*	to indicate.
	v.	to celebrate.
	v.	to give marks to the students.
	n.	a spot or cut mark.
	n.	a symbol, sign, a target.
Marc	*n.*	left over material after grapes have been used to make wine.
Marque	*n.*	a well known make of a manufactured product.
Marry	*v.*	to get married.
Mary	*n.*	mother of Jesus.
Merry	*adj.*	joyous, cheerful.
Mash	*n.*	a warm food for horses.
	v.	to crush food into soft mass.
Mesh	*n.*	net, web.
Mess	*n.*	disorder.
	n.	room to take meal together.
Mass	*n.*	lots, a large number or amount of sth.
	n.	what sth contains.
	v.	to gather in large number.
Maas	*n.*	amasi, sour milk.

Massage	*n.*	the rubbing of parts of body.
Message	*n.*	information sent.
Mat	*n.*	carpet to cover floor.
Mate	*n.*	friend.
	v.	*(animal & birds)* to have sex.
Matt		(also matte). *adj.* not shiny.
Me	*pron.*	*Object. case* of 'I'.
Mi	*n.*	(*music)*, the third note.
Mean	*adj.*	base, mediocre.
	adj.	not generous.
	v.	*mean, meant, meant.* what one wants to say.
	n.	average *(arithmetic & geometric mean)*
Means	*n.*	agency, resources, wealth.
Mien	*n.*	person's bearing or appearance.
Measure	*n.*	size, unit.
	v.	to assess.
Major	*n.*	an army officer next above captain.
	adj.	greater, more important.
Mead	*n.*	a sweet alcoholic drink.
Meed	*n.*	reward.
Mid	*adj.*	middle.
Meat	*n.*	animal flesh taken as food.
Meet	*v.*	*meet, met, met.* come into contact with.
	adj.	fit or suitable.
Mensuration	*n.*	the act of measuring.
Menstruation	*n.*	when a female menstruates.
Meter	*n.*	a device for measuring.
Metre	*n.*	*abbre: m.* unit for measuring length.
	n.	verse rhythm.
Métier	*n.*	a person's work.
Might	*aux.*	*p.t.* of *may.* used to express strength, power, remote possibility etc.
	adv.	power.
Mite	*n.*	a very small insect.
	n.	a small amount.

Minister	*n.*	clergyman.
	n.	minister in the government.
Minster	*n.*	a large or important church.
Ministerial	*adj.*	related to ministry or minister.
Minstrel	*n.*	bard, poet.
Mint	*n.*	a plant with dark green leaves *(podina).*
	n.	a place where money is made.
Meant	*v.*	*mean, meant, meant.* to mean.
A mint	*n.*	a large amount of money.
Mis	*pref.*	in the sense of bad, wrong.
Miss	*v.*	failure to hit.
	v.	escape.
	n.	a young unmarried girl.
Modal	*adj.*	the word which express the mode of action.
	n.	denoted by main verb.
Model	*n.*	a pattern an ideal, a copy of sth.
	n.	a person who advertises a product.
Module	*n.*	part of a course of study.
Mode	*n.*	a way of doing sth.
Mowed	*v.*	*mow, mowed, mowed.* to cut grass.
Mole	*n.*	small dark raised spot on the skin.
	n.	small burrowing mammal.
	n.	a protected harbour.
	n.	unit of amount of substance.
Mall	*n.*	shopping mall.
Moll	*n.*	the female friend of a criminal.
Mop	*n.*	an object to clean floors.
	n.	a mass of thick hair.
Mope	*v.*	to be depressed & listless.
Moral	*adj.*	right conduct.
Morale	*n.*	mental state.
Morel	*n.*	an edible fungus.
Mural	*adj.*	painting done on the wall.

Morn	*n.*	morning.
Mourn	*v.*	to lament.
Moss	*n.*	small flowerless plant growing in moisture.
Mosh	*v.*	to dance at a concert.
Mousy	*adj.*	like a mouse.
Mousse	*n.*	dish of flavoured cream.
Mule	*n.*	an animal which carries loads.
	n.	a slipper.
Mull	*n.*	a muddle.
	n.	a soft muslin.
	v.	to think over, consider.
	v.	to heat wine with spices & sugar.
Mum	*adj.*	silent.
Mum, Mom	*n.*	a mother
Mumm	*v.*	to mask.
Mush	*n.*	porridge.
Muss	*v.*	to disorganize.
Mustard	*n.*	yellow condiment.
Mustered	*v.*	gathered.
Naval	*adj.*	connected with navy, marine.
Navel	*n.*	the middle of the abdomen.
Navvy	*n.*	labourer working on road etc.
Navy	*n.*	branch of armed forces.
Need	*n.*	necessity, want.
Knead	*v.*	to press & stretch flour, clay etc.
Neigh	*adv.*	almost, nearly.
Nigh	*v.*	sound by a horse.
Ness	*n.*	head land *(antreep).*
Ness	*suff.*	the quality, state or character of.
Never	*adv.*	not ever.
Neighbour	*n.*	one who lives next door.
Nil	*n.*	nothing.
Nill	*v.*	not to like.

Nice	*adj.*	fine, pleasant, kind, subtle.
Niece	*n.*	daughter of brother or sister.
Niche	*n.*	a comfortable position, a nook.
Knees	*n.*	*plu* of *knee.*
Noble	*adj.*	loft, great, splendid.
	n.	a person of high social rank.
Nobel Prize	*n.*	one of six international prizes given by Noble Foundation.
Nobble	*v.*	to obtain unfairly.
Novel	*adj.*	new, peculiar, unusual.
	n.	a fiction, imaginary long story book.
Noisy	*adj.*	full of noise.
Nosy, Nosey	*adj.*	interested in unconcerned things.
Non	*pref.*	not.
None	*pron.*	no one, not any.
Nun	*n.*	a holy woman who lives in convent.
Oar	*n.*	pole with a flat blade for rowing.
Or	*conj.*	*& prep.* introducing an alternative.
	suff.	a person or thing that.
Ore	*n.*	metal ore.
Odd	*adj.*	not even.
Odds	*n.*	*plu.* inequality.
Ode	*n.*	a lyric poem.
Odour (also odor)	*n.*	a pleasant smell.
Ordure	*n.*	faeces.
Of	*prep.*	relating to, from, out of, stating the possessor.
Off	*adv.*	away, out of position, separate.
On	*prep.*	upon, at near, in addition to, as a result of.
One	*adj.*	single, certain, same.
	det.	the number: 1, the most important one.
Own	*n.*	of oneself.
	v.	to possess, to have sth.
Own	*adj,*	*pron.* that the thing belongs to sb.
Won	*v.*	*win, won, won.*
Awn	*n.*	the slender sharp hair of corn.

Operation	*n.*	cutting open a part of body as a treatment.
	n.	military or organized activity.
Oppression	*n.*	cruel & unfair treatment.
Ordinance	*n.*	a law.
Ordnance	*n.*	military weapons & ammunitions.
Our	*det.*	*(poss. pron of we)* belonging to us.
Hour	*n.*	60 minutes.
Outer	*adj.*	external.
Outré	*adj.*	very unusual.
Otter	*n.*	a small water loving animal.
Oven	*n.*	heated container for cooking.
Woven	*v.*	*weave, wove, woven.*
Overdo	*n*	to do to excess.
Overdue	*adj.*	past due.
Overseas	*adj.*	abroad.
Oversee	*v.*	supervise
Owe	*v.*	to be in debt.
Woe	*n.*	grief, sorrow, a curse.
Woo	*v.*	to try to get the support of sb, to court.
Pad	*n.*	cushion.
Paid	*v.*	*pt. & pp.* of *pay.*
Pail	*n.*	an open vessel for carrying water etc.
Pal	*n.*	a close friend.
Pale	*n.*	stake, enclosure.
	adj.	dim.
Pall	*n.*	a black cloth laid over coffin at a funeral.
	v.	to make or become tedious.
Pain	*n.*	bodily or mental suffering.
Pan	*n.*	a broad pot used in cooking.
	pref.	denoting total.
	comb. form.	including all of sth.
Pane	*n.*	plate of glass in window.
Paint	*n.*	powder to be mixed in liquid to colour sth.
Pant	*v.*	to breathe fast.
Pants	*n.*	trousers.
Pent	*adj.*	confined, shut in.

Pair	*n.*	two things of a kind.
Pear	*n.*	a fruit.
Peer	*n.*	a person of equal status.
Pier	*n.*	landing stage, pillar supporting a bridge.
Palate	*n.*	the top part of the inside of mouth.
Palette	*n.*	a thin board used by artists.
Pallet	*n.*	a heavy metal base for storing food.
Palm	*n.*	the inner surface of the hand.
	n.	a branchless tropical tree *(taad).*
	v.	to conceal in palm.
Pam	*n.*	the knave of clubs at loo.
Panel	*n.*	a provision of metal that is part of the outer.
	n.	frame.
	n.	group of specialists.
Penal	*adj.*	of or as legal punishment.
Paper	*n.*	sheet for writing.
Pepper	*n.*	an aromatic pungent spice.
Par	*n.*	equality of value.
Per	*pref.*	all over, completely, very.
Per	*prep.*	by means of, for every.
Purr	*n*	sound of cat.
Parameter	*n.*	set of fixed limits.
Perimeter	*n.*	the outer limits.
Parch	*v.*	to roast.
Perch	*n.*	a fresh water fish.
	n.	sitting place for birds.
Parish	*n.*	an area that has its own church.
Perish	*v.*	to be lost or destroyed.
Parol	*adj.*	oral *(law).*
Parole	*n.*	an agreement for release of prisoner before time.
Pat	*v.*	to tap gently.
Pate	*n.*	the head.
Pet	*n.*	tamed animal.
Patrol	*v.*	*& n.* to keep guard by moving here & there.
Petrol	*n.*	substance used as fuel.

Patter	*n.*	a sound of many quick light taps.
Peter	*v.*	gradually decrease & cease.
Pause	*v.*	to stop for some time.
Pose	*v.*	to create a threat, problem etc.
	v.	to give a position for photograph.
	n.	affectation.
Pea	*n.*	a green vegetable.
Pee	*v.*	to urinate.
Peace	*n.*	calm.
Piece	*n.*	a fragment, a portion.
Peak	*n.*	height, top of a mountain.
Peek	*v.*	to peep.
Pick	*n.*	a sharp pointed tool.
	v.	to dig, to uplift.
Peal	*n.*	a loud sound of bells.
Peel	*v.*	to strip of the skin of fruit etc.
Pill	*n.*	a small ball of medicine.
Pearl	*n.*	a gem.
Purl	*n.*	a stitch used in knitting.
Pedal	*n.*	a foot operated lever.
Peddle	*v.*	to sell goods by moving.
Pie	*n.*	a mag pie, species of wood pecker.
	n.	fruit baked in a dish.
	n.	a printing type indiscriminately mixed.
	n.	a coin, small amount.
Pi	*n.*	*(geometry)* symbol.
Place	*n.*	position, point or area.
Plaice	*n.*	flat sea fish.
Plain	*adj.*	clear, simple, easy.
	n.	a large area of flat land.
Plane	*n.*	an aero plane.
Plantar	*n.*	foot sole.
Planter	*n.*	owner of a plantation.
Plait	*n.*	a fold, a braid of hair.
Plate	*n.*	a sheet of metal, dish.

Plum	*n.*	a fruit.
Plume	*n.*	a feather, a crest on helmet.
Plough	*n.*	a implement for ploughing field.
Plow	*v.*	to plough.
Pock	*n.*	pustule of small pox.
Poke	*v.*	to quickly push any object.
Police	*n.*	the civil force to maintain public order.
Polish	*v.*	to make smooth & glossy.
	n.	substance to make surface shiny.
Polish	*n.*	language or people of Poland.
Pop	*n.*	a sudden explosive sound.
	n.	modern popular music.
Pope	*n.*	the head of Roman Catholic Church.
Poplar	*n.*	a tall tree with soft wood.
Popular	*adj.*	famous.
Poppet	*n.*	sb liked or loved.
Puppet	*n.*	*kathputali.*
Pottie	*n.*	a small basket.
Potty	*adj.*	insignificant.
Pour	*v.*	to flow or cause to flow.
Poor	*adj.*	helpless, having little or no money.
Pore	*n.*	a tiny opening, to study sth closely.
Pure	*adj.*	unmixed, blameless, chaste.
Practice	*n.*	habitual action, custom.
	n.	when doctors or lawyers work it is called practice.
Practise	*v.*	to do again & again in order to become perfect.
Prawn	*n.*	a shellfish.
Prone	*adj.*	liable, prostrate.
Pray	*v.*	to worship God; to implore.
Prey	*n.*	victim.
Preview	*n.*	previous review.
Purview	*n.*	range, scope, intention.

Prier	*n.*	one who searches.
Prior	*n.*	a monk.
	adj.	previous.
Principal	*adj.*	most important, chief.
	n.	head of a school or college.
	n.	sum of money originally borrowed or lent.
Principle	*n.*	rule to guide moral conduct.
Prize	*n.*	a reward.
	adj.	treasure.
Pries	*adj.*	looks closely.
Prise	*v.*	to use force to separate sth from sth else.
Pros	*n.*	professional.
Prose	*n.*	literature.
Prove	*v.*	to test, to verify, to examine.
Probe	*n.*	investigation.
Pull	*v.*	to draw towards one.
Pool	*n.*	a pond.
Pule	*v.*	to chirp, to whine.
Pus	*n.*	matter of an ulcer.
Puss	*n.*	a cat, a hare, a tiger.
Quack	*n.*	the sound a duck makes.
	n.	a person practicing medicine without proper knowledge or skill of it.
Quake	*v.*	tremble.
Quarts	*n.*	unit of liquid measure.
Quartz	*n.*	mineral.
Quarry	*n.*	mines.
	n.	prey.
Query	*n.*	an enquiry about sth.
	n.	a question mark to show why the task has not been accomplished.
Quaver	*v.*	to shake, to vibrate.
Quiver	*n.*	a case for arrows.
	v.	to shiver.

Quell	*v.*	calm.
Quill	*n.*	pointed spines of porcupines.
Quiet	*adj.*	calm, still.
Quite	*adv.*	entirely, altogether.
Ragging	*n.*	to play trick on sb.
Rigging	*n.*	the ropes supporting the masts & sails of ship.
Rap	*n.*	a sharp blow or criticism, a punishment.
	n.	a type of music.
Wrap	*n.*	a piece of covering.
Rape	*v.*	to carry away by force.
	n.	sexual intercourse with a woman against her will.
	n.	turnip like plant.
Wrap	*v.*	to cover, to conceal.
Rat	*n.*	a mouse.
Rats	*excl.*	used to show anger.
Rate	*n.*	proportion, tax, cost.
	n.	measurement of the speed.
	v.	rank, merit.
Rete, Rait	*v.*	to soak in water to soften.
Raw	*adj.*	not cooked or manufactured, inexperienced.
Roe	*n.*	a deer of small variety.
Row	*n.*	line, rank.
	v.	to ferry boat.
Read	*v.*	to study.
Reed	*n.*	a plant with hollow stem.
Rid	*v.*	to make free.
Read	*v.*	*p.t* & *p.p.* of *read.*
Red	*n.*	a colour.
Ready	*adj.*	prepared, willing.
Reedy	*adj.*	full of reeds.
Reason	*n.*	cause, motif.
Region	*n.*	tract of land.
	n.	a part of the body usually one that has a particular character or problem.
Recede	*v.*	to move back.
Reseed	*v.*	to seed again.

Recent	*adj.*	that happened a short time ago.
Resent	*v.*	to feel bitter or angry about sth.
Resent	*v.*	sent again.
Refer	*v.*	to send back for information.
Reefer	*n.*	a type of woolen jacket.
Reefer	*n.*	a person who reefs *(covers sails).*
Refuge	*n.*	shelter.
Refuse	*v.*	to turn down, deny.
Refuse	*n.*	waste matter, rubbish, garbage.
Regrate	*v.*	to buy & sell in the same market due to which
	v.	prices rise up.
Regret	*v.*	to repent.
Reins	*n.*	the kidneys.
Reign	*n.*	supremacy, rule.
Rein	*n.*	a controlling or restraining influence.
Wren	*n.*	a very small bird.
Rest	*v.*	to stop doing, to sleep.
	n.	repose, leisure.
	n.	remainder.
Wrest	*v.*	wrench.
Retail	*n.*	sale of commodities one by one.
Retell	*v.*	to tell again.
Retch		vomit.
Wretch		scoundrel.
Revel	*v.*	make merry.
Rebel	*n.*	mutineer.
Revere	*v.*	to respect.
Reverie	*n.*	day dreaming.
Right	*adj.*	correct, proper.
	n.	legal claim to have sth.
	n.	*opp.* of left *(side).*
	v.	return to position.
Rite	*n.*	rituals.
Riot	*n.*	uproar, disturbance of public peace.
Ryot	*n.*	cultivator.

Write	*v.*	to set down in writing.
Wright	*n.*	a workman.
Ring	*n.*	circular band worn on the finger.
	n.	a small hoop.
	v.	to make sound of bell.
Wring	*v.*	*wrung, wrung.* to twist & squeeze clothes when washed.
Road	*n.*	a public path.
Rode	*v.*	*p.t.* of *ride.*
	v.	to fly in the evening.
Rod	*n.*	a slender stick or metal bar.
Rowed	*v.*	*row, rowed, rowed.* to ferry boat.
Roaster	*n.*	one that roasts.
Roster	*n.*	a list of duties turn wise.
Rob	*v.*	to commit robbery.
Robe	*n.*	garment.
Rove	*v.*	roam.
Role	*n.*	part of an actor in a play.
Roll	*n.*	rolled cloth, paper etc.
	v.	to revolve.
Root	*n.*	the underground part of plant, base.
Rout	*n.*	disorderly fight.
Route	*n.*	a way, a course.
Rose	*n.*	a flower.
	v.	*rise, rose, risen.*
Rows	*n.*	horizontal line of sth.
Rote	*n.*	frequent repetition of speech.
Rot	*v.*	*& n.* decay, nonsense.
Wrote	*v.*	*p.t.* of *write.*
Wrought	*v.*	caused sth to happen.
Rude	*adj.*	impolite.
Rued	*v.*	*rue, rued, rued.* regret.
Ruler	*n.*	one who rules or governs.
	n.	a straight strip for measuring or drawing.
Rural	*adj.*	connected with country side.

Run away	*adj.*	having left without telling any one.
Runway	*n.*	a passage to take off the aircraft.
Rummer	*n.*	a large drinking glass.
Rumour	*n.*	an unverified report.
Roomer	*n.*	a person who rents room in sb's house.
Rye	*n.*	seed from grain.
Wry	*adj.*	ironic.
Saber	*n.*	(also saber) a sword.
Sever	*v.*	to cut.
Shaver	*n.*	an electric shaving device.
Safe	*n.*	cupboard to keep valuables.
	adj.	unharmed, secure.
Shape	*v.*	to give a form, to plan.
Sail	*n.*	piece of canvas used in ships.
	v.	to travel by sea.
Sale	*n.*	act of selling.
Shale	*n.*	a type of soft stone.
Saint	*n.*	a holy man.
Scent	*n.*	fragrance.
Sent	*v.*	*send, sent, sent.* to make sth go.
Salient	*adj.*	most important, noticeable.
Silent	*adj.*	quiet.
Sallow	*n.*	a tree or shrub like willow.
Shallow	*adj.*	not deep.
Same	*adj.*	identical, uniform.
Sham	*v.*	to pretend.
	n.	thing or person that is not genuine.
Shame	*n.*	feeling of humiliation.
Sandy	*adj.*	covered with sand.
Shandy	*n.*	drink made of beer & lemonade.
Sank	*v.*	*sink, sank, sunk.* to submerge, fade.
Shank	*n.*	leg part between ankle & knee.
Sat	*v.*	*p.t. & p.p.* of *sit.*
Sate	*v.*	to suffice.

Satire	*n.*	mockery, ridicule.
Satyr	*n.*	a goat shaped wood land deity.
Save	*v.*	to protect.
Shave	*v.*	to remove hair with a razor.
Saving	*n.*	money saved.
Shaving	*v.*	*shave, shaving.*
Shavings	*n.*	thin pieces cut from wood.
Saw	*n.*	a cutting tool with toothed edge.
	n.	saying, maxim.
	v.	*p.t. sawed, p.p. sawn, sawed,* to use a saw to cut sth.
	v.	*see, saw, seen.*
Shaw	*n.*	a thicket.
Scarf	*n.*	a cloth worn by women on head, neck etc.
Scarp	*n.*	perpendicular.
Scent	*n.*	smell, fragrance.
	v.	to perceive by smell.
Sent	*v.*	*p.t. & p.p.* of *send.*
Cent	*n.*	a coin.
Scissor	*v.*	to cut with scissors.
Scissors	*n.*	a cutter with two pivoted blades.
Seizor	*n.*	one that seizes.
Seizur	*n.*	act of seizing.
Score	*n.*	number won, an incision.
	v.	to succeed, to make a cut or mark on a surface.
Scour	*v.*	to comb, to search sth.
Scrap	*n.*	shred, fragment.
Scrape	*v.*	to make grating noise.
	n.	difficult situation.
Scull	*n.*	a small oar rowing boat.
Skull	*n.*	the bone of head.
Sea	*n.*	wide extend of salt water.
See	*v.*	to behold, to visit, to witness.
	n.	the office of a Bishop.
She	*pron.*	the *opp* of *he.*
	n.	a female animal.
S/he	*pron.*	used when it is not clear that the subject is *she* or *he.*

Seal	*n.*	a sea animal.
	v.	to put a seal.
	v.	to close sth.
Seel	*v.*	to render blind.
Ceil	*v.*	to cover the inner roof.
Seam	*n.*	a line formed by the sewing.
Seem	*v.*	to appear to be.
Shim	*n.*	a piece of sth to fill a space.
Sim	*n.*	a computer or video games.
SIM	*n.*	a plastic card inside a mobile phone.
Seating	*n.*	seats.
Sitting	*n.*	sittings of a court or parliament.
	v.	sit, sat, sat, sitting.
Secrete	*v.*	to produce fluids.
Secret	*adj.*	hidden, secluded.
Seen	*v.*	*see, saw, seen.*
Scene	*n.*	a performance on the stage.
	n.	view.
Seine	*n.*	fishing net.
Sheen	*n.*	shine.
Seep	*v.*	to ooze, trickle.
Sheep	*n.*	a grass eating animal.
Sheaf	*n.*	a bundle of papers tied together.
	n.	a bunch of cut stalks of grain.
Seethe	*v.*	to boil.
Sheath	*n.*	the scabbard.
Sheathe	*v*	to put into sheath.
Seize	*v.*	to get hold of.
Size	*n.*	extend, volume.
Cease	*v.*	to stop, to cut short.
Self	*n.*	one's individual person.
	adj.	absorbed by one's own interest.
Self	*pref.*	of or by oneself or itself, automatically.
Shelf	*n.*	a slab in the wall for putting sth.
Serf	*n.*	slave.
Surf	*n.*	breaking waves.

Serge	*n.*	woolen twilled stuff.
Surge	*n.*	a large wave.
Cerge	*n.*	a large wax candle burned before the altar.
Serif	*n.*	the short cross line at the end of printing type.
Sheriff	*n.*	the chief officer of a shire.
Serous	*adj.*	thin, watery.
Serious	*adj.*	grave, earnest, dangerous.
Seven	*number.*	six plus one.
Shaven	*adj.*	with hair removed.
Sever	*v.*	cut sth, to separate.
Severe	*adj.*	strict or harsh.
Shade	*n.*	darkness due to cutting of rays of light.
Said	*v.*	*say, said, said.*
She'd		*short form* she had, she would.
Shed	*v.*	to let or have fall of.
	n.	roofed shelter.
Shamble	*v.*	to walk slowly.
Symbol	*n.*	a sign of sth.
Cymbal	*n.*	hollow of a vessel.
Shear	*v.*	*sheared, shorn.* to cut wool of a sheep.
Sear	*v.*	scorch.
	adj.	very sharp.
Seer	*n.*	prophet.
Sere		*(also sear) adj.* dried up withered.
Share	*v.*	divide among people.
	n.	portion or claim as one's due.
	n.	blade of a plough.
Shears	*n.*	a garden scissors.
Sheer	*adj.*	pure, mere.
	v.	to deviate from proper course.
Cere	*v.*	to cover with wax.
Sheave	*n.*	a grooved wheel.
Sieve	*n.*	utensil for filtering.
Sheet	*n.*	a piece of linen or metal.
	n.	rope for controlling the position of sail.
Seat	*n.*	a thing to sit on.

Shift	*v.*	to move.
	v.	get rid of.
	n.	a period of time worked.
	n.	a system on a computer keyboard.
Sift	*v*	to put flour through a sieve.
Shingle	*n.*	small flat wood to cover the roof.
	v.	to cut the hair very close.
Shingles	*n.*	a disease of nerves.
Single	*adj.*	one, not married.
Ship	*n.*	a vessel.
	v.	to be available to be bought.
	suff.	the state or quality of.
Sip	*v.*	to drink sth.
Shire	*n.*	a county.
Sire	*n.*	father, male ancestor, title of king.
Shock	*n.*	a violent concussion.
	n.	shaggy hair.
Soak	*v.*	to drench, to absorb.
Sock	*n.*	a light stocking.
	n.	plough share.
Shocker	*n.*	vulgar & exciting tale.
Soccer	*n.*	football play.
Shod	*v.*	*shoe, shod, shod.*
Sod	*n.*	a turf.
Shoe	*n.*	covering for the foot.
	n.	a part of a brake.
Shoo	*interj.*	go away.
Shook	*v.*	*shake, shook, shaken.* to move.
Sook	*n.*	a coward.
Shoot	*v.*	to fire a weapon.
	n.	new part that grows on a plant.
	n.	film shooting.
Suit	*n.*	petition, wooing, set of clothes.
Suite	*n.*	retinue, a set of rooms.
Soot	*n.*	a black substance caused by smoke.

Shooter	*n.*	who or which shoots.
Suitor	*n.*	a match for a woman.
Shone	*v.*	*shine, shone, shone.*
Shown	*v.*	*show, showed, shown.*
Sown	*v.*	*sow, sowed, sown.*
Shop	*n.*	a place for selling items.
Soap	*n.*	washing or bathing material.
Sop	*n.*	piece of bread etc. soaked in milk.
Short	*adj,*	*adv. & noun.* not long or tall.
Shorts	*n.*	short trousers.
Sort	*n.*	kind, class, manner.
Shoulder	*n.*	parts of the body at the top of each arm & neck.
	v.	to accept the responsibility for sth.
Soldier	*n.*	military man.
	v.	to continue with the task.
Solder	*v.*	to join two metals by soldering.
Sick	*adj.*	ill.
	v.	to vomit.
Sic	*adv.*	so thus.
Chic	*n.*	style & elegance.
Sics	*v.*	attacks.
Six	*n.*	five plus one.
Sign	*n.*	a mark, symbol, signature.
Shin	*n.*	bony front of the lower leg.
Sin	*n.*	an offence against God.
Syn	*pref.*	with, together, at the same time.
Sine	*n.*	*(abbre- sin)* the ratio of the length of side opposite. one of the angles in a right angled triangle.
	prep.	without.
Shine	*v.*	*shone, shone.*
Sinew	*n.*	strong band of tissue in body.
Sinewy	*adj.*	wiry.
Sink	*n.*	to submerge.
Sync	*n.*	to match up.

Sit	*v.*	to be seated.
Shit	*v.*	to evacuate bowels.
Slack	*adj.*	loose slow sluggish.
	n.	a dull period.
	v.	to work less hard than usual.
Slake	*v.*	quench.
Slander	*n.*	false spoken statement.
Slender	*adj.*	slim.
Cylinder	*n.*	a solid or hollow figure with round & long straight sides.
Slay	*v.*	to kill.
Sley	*n.*	a weaver's reed.
Sleight	*n.*	a sledge.
	adj.	cunning, skill.
Slight	*n.*	slender.
Slop	*n.*	a policeman.
	n.	dirty water of a household.
Slope	*n.*	uneven ground.
Slops	*n.*	trousers.
Slough	*n.*	muddy place.
	n.	the cast skin of serpent.
Slow	*adj.*	not fast, sluggish.
	adv.	slowly.
	v.	to make less active.
Sloe	*n.*	a fruit, black thorn.
Smock	*n.*	a woman's undergarments.
Smoke	*n.*	vaporous matter arising from burning substance.
Smoother	*adj.*	*smooth, smoother, smoothest.* completely flat & even.
Smother	*v.*	to suffocate, to suppress.
Snack	*n.*	a slight hasty meal.
Snake	*n.*	a serpent.
Soar	*v.*	to fly or mount aloft.
Shore	*n.*	the coast.
Sore	*adj.*	painful, sad, annoyed.

	n.	wound.
	adv.	severely, greatly.
Swore	*v.*	*p.t.* of *swear.*
Soon	*adv.*	early, quickly.
Swoon	*v.*	faint.
Sooth	*n.*	truth, reality.
Soothe	*v.*	to calm.
	v.	firmly fixed on truth.
Soul	*n.*	non material part of a person.
Shoal	*n.*	large number of fish swimming together.
	n.	small hill of sand bank.
	v.	to crowd, to become shallow.
Sol	*n.*	the fifth note of major scale.
Sole	*n.*	the base of shoes, bottom of a thing.
	adj.	only, single.
Sour	*adj.*	having a pungent taste.
	adj.	not cheerful.
Shower	*n.*	a brief fall of rain or snow.
	v.	to drop a lot of small things onto sb.
Sower	*n.*	one that sows.
Sow	*v.*	to scatter seed in the ground.
	v.	to spread feelings in sb's mind.
	n.	a female pig.
Show	*v.*	to display.
	n.	an exhibition, display.
So	*adv.*	in that manner, thus, to that degree.
Sough	*v.*	to make a soft whistling sound *(wind).*
Spat	*v.*	*p.p.* of *spit.*
Spate	*n.*	sudden flood in river.
Spear	*n.*	a long pointed weapon.
Spare	*v.*	to let off, to refrain from using.
Sphere	*n.*	globe, planet.
Spec	*n.*	speculation.
Specs	*n.*	pair of spectacles.
Speck	*n.*	a small spot.

Spirit	*n.*	mind, feelings & character together.
	n.	courage, determination.
	n.	soul, a ghost.
	n.	strong alcoholic drink.
Esprit	*n.*	liveliness or wit.
Sprite	*n.*	an apparition, an elf, a fairy.
Square	*n.*	figure with four equal sides and four right angles.
	n.	an open space in a town.
	n.	the product of a number multiplied by itself.
	adv.	directly.
Squire	*n.*	a man next in rank to knight.
Stack	*n.*	ordered pile, large amount.
Stake	*n.*	a pointed stick or post driven into the ground.
	n.	money wagered.
	v.	to support, to risk money, to bet.
The stake	*n.*	a post to punish criminals.
Stager	*n.*	a person having rich experience.
Stagger	*v.*	to reel, to affect strongly as with sorrow.
Stair	*n.*	one of series of steps.
Stare	*v.*	to gaze.
Steer	*n.*	a young ox.
	v.	to direct the course of a ship etc.
Stir	*v.*	to move spoon, to excite.
State	*n.*	condition, rank.
	n.	free civil community.
	v.	to write or say sth.
Estate	*n.*	a piece of landed property.
Stationary	*adj.*	not in motion, stable.
Stationery	*n.*	writing material.
Steal	*v.*	to commit theft.
Steel	*n.*	a hard metal, a sword.
Steam	*n.*	watery vapour, energy.
Esteem	*n.*	high self opinion.
Stile	*n.*	passageway.
Style	*adj.*	fashion.

Stoke	*v.*	to add fuel to fire..
Stock	*n.*	an available supply of goods.
Stocks	*n.*	a wooden structure used in the past to punish the criminals.
Stoop	*v.*	to bend down.
	n.	a platform, a porch.
Stop	*v.*	to cease, to halt.
Estop	*v.*	to impede.
Storey	*n.*	one floor of building.
Story	*n.*	tale, legend.
History	*n.*	systematic record of past events.
Strait	*adj.*	narrow, strict, difficult.
	n.	a narrow area of sea connecting larger sea.
Straight	*adj.*	without curves.
Straits	*n.*	a financial crisis.
Strip	*v.*	to undress, dismantle.
	n.	long piece of paper, metal, cloth etc.
Strip	*n.*	a street that has many shops.
Stripe	*n.*	a long narrow band or line of colour.
Succour	*v.*	help sb.
Sucker	*n.*	a person easily tricked or persuaded.
Sun	*n.*	the brightest celestial body.
	v.	to bask in the sun.
Shun	*v.*	to avoid, to refrain from.
Son	*n.*	a male child.
Swoon	*v.*	to faint.
Soon	*adv.*	in a short time, promptly.
Symmetry	*n.*	similarity.
Cemetery	*n.*	burial place people.
Tacks	*n.*	short nails.
Tax	*n.*	amount of income paid to govt.
Tail	*n.*	an appendage of an animal.
	n.	ownership limited to a person or his heirs.
Tale	*n.*	a story.
Teil	*n.*	the lime tree.
Tell	*v.*	to say, to relate.

Talc	*n.*	a fine soft powder.
Talk	*v.*	to converse.
	n.	conversation.
Tawer	*n.*	a dresser of white leather.
Tower	*n.*	a lofty narrow building.
Tea	*n.*	a drink.
Tee	*n.*	a metallic umbrella crowning *pagoda.*
	n.	a flat area on a golf course.
Teak	*n.*	a tropical tree having costly wood.
Teal	*n.*	a web footed water bird.
Tick	*n.*	a beat of watch or clock.
Till	*n.*	money box in a shop.
	v.	to cultivate *(land).*
	prep.	to the time of, until.
	conj.	to the time that.
	n.	cash register.
Team	*n.*	group of players in game.
Teem	*v.*	to abound.
Teathe	*n.*	the manure or dung left on lands by livestock.
Teeth	*plu.*	of *tooth.*
Teethe	*v.*	growing of teeth in a baby' mouth.
Tern	*n.*	a sea swallow.
Turn	*v.*	to divert, to change.
	n.	revolution, new trend.
	n.	opportunity.
Than	*conj. & prep.*	expressing comparison.
Then	*adv, conj & adj.*	at that time, after that.
The	*definite article.*	used to refer to sb/sth that has already been mentioned or is easily understood.
	adj.	indicating particular person or thing.
Thee	*pron.*	*objective & dative case* of *thou.*
Their	*adj. or pron.*	of them.
There	*adv.*	in, to or that place.
Theirs	*pron.*	*(used without nouns).*
Thorough	*adj.*	complete, entire.
Through	*prep, adv & adj.*	from one end or side of another.

Throw	*v.*	*threw, thrown.* to fling.
Thro	*contraction* of *through.*	
Throes	*n.*	violent pain.
Though	*adv. &conj.*	although, despite the fact that
Tide	*n.*	ebb & flow of the ocean.
Tied	*v.*	*tie, tied, tied.*
To	*prep.*	in direction of, towards.
Toe	*n.*	foot's thickest digit.
Too	*adv.*	also, in addition, as well, excessively.
Tow	*v.*	to pull a car or boat behind another vehicle using a chain.
Two	*adj. & n.*	the sum of one & one.
Tongs	*n.*	a device used for grasping & lifting.
Tongue	*n.*	fleshy muscular organ in mouth.
Top	*n.*	the highest park, rank or position.
Tope	*v.*	to drink to excess.
	v.	mango or other grove.
Trade	*n.*	commercial, business.
Tread	*v.*	to step on, to trample, to subdue.
Trek	*v.*	to travel far on foot.
Track	*n.*	a way, a railway line.
Tri	*pref.*	signifying three.
Try	*n.*	attempt.
	v.	to make an effort to sth.
Troop	*n.*	a group of scouts or soldiers.
Troupe	*n.*	a company of actors or performers.
Van	*n.*	a covered vehicle for goods.
Vane	*n.*	a weather cock, the blade of wind mill.
Vain	*adj.*	useless.
Vein	*n.*	a blood vessel.
Vary	*v.*	to change, to be different.
Very	*adj.*	true, real, actual.
	adv.	in a high degree, absolutely, truly.
Vent	*n.*	a hole, an exit.
Bent	*v.*	*p.t & p.p.* of *bend.*

Verb	*n.*	a part of speech that denotes what a person or thing does.
Verve	*n.*	enthusiasm, vigour
Verses	*n.*	lines of poetry.
Versus	*n.*	against.
Virtu	*n.*	love for fine arts.
Virtue	*n.*	moral goodness, advantage, quality.
Voe	*n.*	a bay.
Vow	*n.*	an oath.
Wad	*n.*	a pad of paper in gun.
Wade	*v.*	to walk through water.
Wail	*n.*	moan.
Whale	*n.*	a very large sea animal.
Wait	*v.*	to stay for.
Weight	*n.*	how heavy is sth.
Wet	*v.*	soaked with water.
Whet	*v.*	to sharpen or increase.
Waive	*v.*	to put off.
Wave	*n.*	movement in the sea water.
	v.	to move hand in the air.
Weave	*v.*	to make cloth, carpet, basket etc by crossing threads.
Wan	*adj.*	pale, gloomy.
Wane	*n.*	decline, decrease.
Ware	*n.*	manufactured articles.
Were	*v.*	the *plu.* of *was* used as *p.t.* of *be.*
Wear	*v.*	to dress.
We're	*short form.*	we are.
Where	*adv.*	at which or in what place.
Way	*n.*	method or manner of doing sth.
	n.	route or road, direction.
	adv.	very far, by a large amount.
Weigh	*v.*	to measure weight.
Web	*n.*	net spun by spider.
The Web	*n.*	World Wide Web.

Wee	*adj.*	small, little.
We	*plu.*	of 'I', people in general.
Week	*n.*	a period of seven days.
Weak	*adj.*	feeble, unsound, frail.
West	*n.*	*opp* of *east.*
Waist	*n.*	the part of a human body.
Waste	*adj.*	uncultivated, barren, discarded.
	v.	to devastate, to misuse.
Wet	*adj.*	covered with liquid.
Whet	*v.*	to sharpen or increase.
Wether	*n.*	custard ram.
Weather	*n.*	the atmospheric condition.
Whether	*pron. & conj.*	which of two *(if).*
Whither	*adv.*	to what or which place.
Wither	*v.*	to fade.
Which	*pron.*	to ask for or to refer to.
Witch	*n.*	woman practicing sorcery.
Wholly	*n.*	entirely, completely.
Holy	*n.*	religious.
Wood	*n.*	a hard material out of tree.
Woods	*n.*	forest.
	n.	a golf club.
Would	*modal verb.*	*p.t.* of *will.* used to express polite
	n.	request, past habit, unreal condition etc.
	adj.	tending to be.
Word	*n.*	meaningful group of letters.
	v.	to express in words.
World	*n.*	universe, creation, earth, people in general.
Wold	*n.*	uncultivated region.
Wreath	*n.*	a ring shaped arrangement of flowers etc.
Wreathe	*v.*	to encircle.
Write-off	*n.*	sth is to acknowledge its complete loss.
Right off	*n.*	immediately, right away.

Yoke	*n.*	a wooden board put on the neck of two oxen
	n.	engaged in ploughing.
Yolk	*n.*	yellow part of an egg.
Yore	*n.*	long since, old times.
Your	*pron.*	*poss.* of you.
	adj.	of you.
Ewer	*n.*	a large jug.
You	*pron.*	
Ewe	*n.*	a female sheep.
Yule	*n.*	the festival of Christmas.
You'll		*short form* you will.
Zest	*n.*	relish, interest.
Jest	*n.*	a joke.
Zoon	*n.*	the total product of a fertilized germ.
June	*n.*	the 6th month of English year.

3

CONFUSING WORDS

Abjure	*v.*	to renounce, reject.
Adjure	*v.*	to appeal.
Ablution	*n.*	washing body before a religious ceremony.
Absolution	*n.*	a freeing from sin, guilt or blame.
Oblation	*n.*	thing offered to God.
Abluvion	*n.*	washed off.
Oblivion	*n.*	forgetfulness.
Aborigine	*n.*	original inhabitant of a region.
Aubergine	*n.*	dark purple tropical fruit.
Abroad	*adv. & adj.* foreign.	
Aboard	*adj.*	on or onto a vehicle.
Abode	*v.*	*p.t.* of *abide.* to live at some place.
	n.	place of residence.
Abscess	*n.*	a swelling containing pus.
Obsess	*v.*	preoccupy compulsively.
Absolute	*adj.*	total & complete.
Obsolete	*adj.*	out of date.
Absorb	*v.*	to take in.
Observe	*v.*	to notice.
Abundant	*adj.*	plentiful.
Redundant	*adj.*	superfluous.

Abuse	*n., v.*	unfair use, insult.
Misuse	*n., v.*	waste, ill-treat.
Accelerate	*v.*	to speed up.
Exhilarate	*v.*	to excite or cause sb feel happy.
Accent	*n.*	emphasis, way of pronouncing words.
Ascent	*n.*	act of climbing or moving up.
Ascend	*n.*	to go up.
Assent	*n.*	consent.
Accept	*v.*	to be agree to receive sth.
Except	*v.*	to leave out, to object.
	prep.	exclusive of.
	conj.	unless.
Expect	*v.*	to hope.
Exempt	*v.*	to excuse or release from an obligation.
Access	*n.*	reach.
Assess	*v.*	to decide or to judge.
Axes	*n.*	*plu* of *axis.* lines round a spinning object, earth's axes.
Excess	*n.*	more than is necessary.
Accidental	*adj.*	happening by chance.
Occidental	*adj.*	belonging to the western part of the world.
Accuse	*v.*	to blame.
Excuse	*n.*	a reason for the wrong done.
Action	*n.*	a thing done by sb.
Auction	*n.*	a public sale of goods or property through bids.
Acute	*adj.*	keen.
Cute	*adj.*	pretty & attractive.
Adage	*n.*	a saying.
Adze	*n.*	a tool for cutting wood.
Adapt	*v.*	to make fit or suitable.
Adept	*adj.*	well skilled.
Adopt	*v.*	to accept.
	v.	to take or claim as own.
Adder	*n.*	a small poisonous snake.
Udder	*n.*	an organ of a mammal from which milk is produced.

Addition	*n.*	act of adding.
Addiction	*n.*	bad habit.
Edition	*n.*	the set of copies published at a time.
Adit	*n.*	access, entrance into a mine.
Audit	*n.*	official examination of financial records, accounts etc.
Edit	*v.*	to arrange & prepare for publication.
Adjacent	*adj.*	near or close *(contact not necessary).*
Adjoining	*adj.*	close *(denotes contact).*
Adult	*n.*	grown up.
Adulterate	*v.*	contaminate.
Adultery	*n.*	sexual unfaithfulness of some one.
Adversary	*n.*	foe, enemy, opponent.
Adversity	*n.*	misfortune, distress.
Adverse	*adj.*	unfavourable.
Averse	*adj.*	strongly disliking.
Afflict	*v.*	to affect in a harmful way.
Inflict	*v.*	to give a blow, pain etc.
Affluence	*n.*	prosperity.
Effluence	*n.*	flowing out.
Influence	*n.*	power, interest, effect.
Opulence	*n.*	luxury, wealth.
Affluent	*adj.*	prosperous.
Effluent	*n.*	liquid discharged as waste.
Opulent	*n.*	impressive or decorated.
Afforest	*v.*	to plant with trees.
Deforest	*v.*	to destroy the trees in a place.
Aft	*adv.*	in the back of ship or aircraft.
After	*prep.*	later than sth or any time.
Again	*adv.*	one more time, on another occasion.
Against	*pref.*	not agreeing with.
Ago	*adj. & adv.*	in the past.
Ego	*n.*	feeling of self importance.

Ailment	*n.*	an illness, disease.
Aliment	*n.*	support, nourishment.
Element	*n.*	the first principle, ingredient.
Alia	*suff.*	things related with a particular activity.
Alias	*n.*	a given name besides the real name.
Alas	*interj.*	expressing sorrow, pity etc.
Alien	*adj.*	hostile, not a citizen.
Align	*v.*	to put sth in the correct position.
A-line	*adj.*	wider at the bottom as compared to the top.
Allay	*v.*	to make less frightened.
Alley	*n.*	a passage.
Ally	*n.*	country supporting another during war.
Aloe	*n.*	a tropical plant with thick leaves.
Alloy	*n.*	a metal made by mixing two or more metals together.
Allude	*v.*	to hint at.
Elude	*v.*	to evade, escape.
Allusion	*n.*	an indirect reference, a hint.
Illusion	*n.*	an untrue idea or belief.
Alone	*adj.*	secluded or without any one.
Along	*prep.*	from one end to other.
Alumina	*n.*	a white substance found in rocks.
Alumna	*n.*	*plu. alumnae.* former female student of an institution.
Alumni	*n.*	the former students.
Alumnus	*n.*	*plu. alumni.* former male student.
Analyse	*v.*	to examine sth.
Analysis	*n.*	*(plu. analyses).* resolution into elements.
Annual	*adj.*	happening once in a year.
Annul	*v.*	declare invalid.
Anterior	*adj.*	earlier, preceding.
Interior	*adj.*	inner, internal.
Apathy	*n.*	lack of feelings
Empathy	*n.*	ability to understand others'feelings by imagining themselves in their situation.
Sympathy	*n.*	to show pity & care for sb's pain, sorrow or condition.

Appalling	*adj.*	horrified.
Appealing	*adj.*	attractive & interesting.
Arise	*v.*	*arose, arisen.* to start, to exist, to get out of bed.
Rise	*n.*	an increase.
	v.	*rose, risen.* get up, to stand up, appearing of sun or moon over horizon.
Art	*n.*	human skill.
	v.	used to mean 'are' usually in poetry.
Artful	*adj.*	cunning.
ASAP	*abbre.*	as soon as possible.
Asp	*n.*	a small poisonous snake.
Assignment	*n.*	a task given to sb.
Assessment	*n.*	evaluation.
Assumption	*n.*	an idea not based on evidence.
Presumption	*n.*	an idea based on evidence.
Assure	*v.*	to give confidence to.
Ensure	*v.*	to guarantee.
Insure	*v.*	to protect by a risk bond.
Atom	*n.*	supposed smallest particle.
Item	*n.*	a single article.
Atomic	*adj.*	pertaining to atoms.
Automatic	*adj.*	self acting.
Attitude	*n.*	posture of body, feeling.
Attribute	*n.*	special quality, a symbol of position.
Altitude	*n.*	height.
Aptitude	*n.*	talent.
Aural	*adj.*	to do with the ear.
Oral	*adj.*	to do with the mouth.
	n.	a spoken exam.
Avid	*adj.*	keen or enthusiastic, greedy.
Ibid		*(referring to a book, page or passage already mentioned).*
	adj.	in the same place.
Avocation	*n.*	a work done besides one's regular work.
Vocation	*n.*	occupation, trade, moral duty.

Babel	*n.*	confusion.
Bad	*adj.*	not good.
Bead	*n.*	small ball used in counting prayers.
Bed	*n.*	used for sleeping on.
B.Ed.	*n.*	*abbr.* Bachelor of Education.
Bubble	*n.*	a small globe of gas that floats in liquid.
Baddy	*n.*	a bad or evil character.
Buddy	*n.*	a friend.
Bade	*v.*	*bid, bade, bidden.*
Badge	*n.*	small piece of metal to show identity.
Bag	*n.*	a small sack, container.
	v.	to put into bag, to win sth, claim sth.
Beg	*v.*	to ask for alms, to implore.
Ballet	*n.*	a performance of dancing on stage.
Ballad	*n.*	a narrative poem.
Ballot	*n.*	ticket used in giving votes.
Valet	*n.*	a personal servant.
Wallet	*n.*	a small folding case.
Banch	*n.*	bench of court.
Bench	*n.*	a long seat.
The bench	*n.*	a judge in the court.
Bangle	*n.*	ring worn around wrist.
Brangle	*v.*	to quarrel.
Barber	*n.*	a person who cuts hair & shaves.
Barbarian	*n.*	uncivilized.
Barock	*n.*	a rough pearl.
Baroque	*adj.*	odd.
Barrack	*n.*	a building for soldiers.
Baste	*v.*	to beat with a stick.
Best	*adj.*	*good, better, best.*
Bath	*n.*	washing of body.
Bathe	*v.*	to take a bath.
Batter	*n.*	a mixture of flour, milk etc.
Better	*adj.*	*comp. degree* of *good.*
Bitter	*adj.*	unpleasant, sharp.

Butter	*n.*	soft milk cream.
	v.	to flatter sb.
Believe	*v.*	to confide in.
Belive	*adv.*	urgently, speedily.
Benefit	*n.*	sth helpful & good as an advantage.
Profit	*n.*	money gained.
Beside	*prep.*	*& adv.* at the side of, near.
Besides	*prep.*	*& adv.* in addition to.
Bless	*v.*	to ask God to protect & bestow his kindness.
Bliss	*n.*	extreme happiness.
Blister	*n.*	small bubble on the skin.
Bluster	*v.*	speak loudly or in a bullying way.
	n.	empty threats or protests.
Bolster	*n.*	a long narrow pillow.
Boast	*v.*	to speak proudly.
Boost	*v.*	to increase or improve sth.
Bonded	*adj.*	mortgaged.
Bounded	*adj.*	restricted.
Bosom	*n.*	a woman's breast.
	n.	a situation in which sb is loved & protected.
Blossom	*n.*	a flower.
	v.	to become healthy.
Breath	*n.*	the air inhaled.
Breathe	*v.*	to inhale air.
Breadth	*n.*	broadness.
Breeze	*n.*	a light wind.
Bridge	*n.*	a road over a river.
Abridge	*v.*	to shorten, to curtail.
Broad	*adj.*	wide.
Brood	*v.*	to think deeply for long time.
	n.	offspring *(birds)* born at the same time.
Brought	*v.*	*bring, brought, brought.* to fetch.
Bought	*v.*	*buy, bought, bought.* to get after paying its price.

Brunt	*n.*	fierce unpleasant shock or attack.
Burnt	*adj.*	spoiled by fire.
	v.	*burn, burnt, burnt.*
Business	*n.*	commercial operations or dealings.
Busyness	*n.*	the state of being busy.
Calendar	*n.*	an almanac.
Calender	*n.*	machine for pressing cloth.
Colander	*n.*	a kitchen container.
Caller	*n.*	a person making a telephone call.
Collar	*n.*	the part of cloth around the neck.
	v.	to capture sb & hold tightly.
Canning	*n.*	process of preserving food stuff in cans.
Cunning	*n.*	craftiness, skill.
	adj.	crafty.
Capital	*n.*	the city from where government functions.
	n.	money.
	n.	larger letter size used in the beginning of the word starting a sentence.
	n.	top part of a pillar.
	adj.	capital punishment.
	adj.	excellent.
Capitol	*n.*	building for US congress.
Capitation	*n.*	a tax or grant per head.
Caption	*n.*	a piece of text in news papers.
Capric	*adj.*	pertaining to the goat.
Caprice	*n.*	a whim, a fancy.
Care	*n.*	attention, worry.
Cure	*n.*	treatment.
Career	*n.*	profession.
Carrier	*n.*	one who or which carries sth.
Courier	*n.*	one who carries messages.
Carnage	*n.*	massacre, bloodshed.
Cranage	*n.*	the fare paid for the use of crane.
Carriage	*n.*	a vehicle, coach.
Courage	*n.*	bravery, fearlessness.

Carve	*v.*	to make figure out of a stone, wood etc.
Curve	*n.*	a bent line.
Celebrate	*v.*	to mark an event.
Celebrity	*n.*	famous person.
Centenary	*n.*	a hundredth anniversary.
Century	*n.*	a hundred.
Centennial	*adj.*	happening once in a hundred year.
Sentinel	*n.*	a soldier set to guard.
Certain	*adj.*	definitely to happen.
Ascertain	*v.*	to make certain.
Cess	*n.*	a rate or tax like education cess.
Chess	*n.*	a game.
Character	*n.*	a letter of the alphabet.
	n.	mental or moral nature.
Corrector	*n.*	a critic, a proof reader.
Cheek	*n.*	either side of the face below the eyes.
	n.	rude behaviour.
Chick	*n.*	a new born hen.
Chin	*n.*	the part of face below the mouth.
Chine	*n.*	the backbone of an animal.
Choral	*adj.*	sung by choir.
Corral	*n.*	a fenced area for horse, cows etc.
Chord	*n.*	the string of a musical instrument.
	n.	chord of a circle.
Cord	*n.*	a thin rope.
Chore	*n.*	a task done regularly.
Core	*n.*	hard central part of fruit.
	adj.	most important, main.
	v.	to take out the core of fruit.
Chose	*v.*	*p.t.* of *choose.*
Chouse	*n.*	a cheat.
Christen	*v.*	to celebrate the naming ceremony of a new born baby.
Christian	*n.*	*adj.* a believer in the religion of Christ.

Civil	*adj.*	the people who live in a country of Christ.
Civilian	*n.*	not a member of the armed forces or the police.
Civility	*n.*	polite behaviour.
Classic	*adj.*	of very best of its kind.
Classical	*n.*	form of traditional in style.
Clause	*n.*	*(grammar)* a part of sentence that has a subject & predicate.
Claws	*n.*	nails of animals or birds.
Close	*v.*	shut, end.
	adj.	near in space or time, almost, likely.
	adv.	not far away.
Cloze-test	*n.*	a type of test.
Claver	*n.*	idle talk.
Clever	*adj.*	skillful.
Cleaver	*n.*	a heavy knife with a broad blade.
Calibre	*n.*	the size of the hole in gun.
(also caliber)	*n.*	a person's ability.
Clean	*adj.*	pure, neat.
	v.	to free from dirt.
Cleanse	*v.*	to make thoroughly clean, to purify.
Click	*n.*	a short sharp sound.
	v.	to press button on a mouse.
Clique	*n.*	a small group of people who spend their time together.
Cliché	*n.*	a phrase or an idea no longer interesting.
Cliff	*n.*	a high area of rock with a very steep side.
Clip	*n.*	a small object for holding things together.
	n.	short part of film shown separately.
	v.	to cut sth with scissors or shears.
	v.	to fasten sth with a clip.
Climactic	*n.*	forming a climax.
Climatic	*adj.*	relating to climate.
Cloth	*n.*	a woven material.
Clothe	*v.*	to dress with clothes.
Coach	*n.*	a trainer.
Couch	*n.*	a carriage, settee.

Coaching	*n.*	special classes or training.
Couching	*n.*	the act of bending.
Coalition	*n.*	a government formed by two or more political parties.
Collation	*n.*	collection of information.
Coarse	*adj.*	rough.
Coerce	*v.*	to compel.
Course	*v.*	to chase.
	n.	the path to move on.
	n.	a series of lessons taught in the schools.
Coast	*n.*	the edge of the sea.
Cost	*n.*	price.
Coat	*n.*	a man's upper garment.
Caught	*v.*	*p.t. & p.p.* of *catch.*
Cote	*n.*	a shelter for animals or birds.
Cot	*n.*	a small, easily movable bed.
Court	*n.*	a small open place, hall of justice.
	v.	to woo.
Cock	*n.*	the male hen.
	v.	to make a gun ready into position for firing.
	v.	to move a part of body
Coke	*n.*	a fuel.
Coffee	*n.*	a drink.
Copy	*n.*	an imitation of an original.
	v.	to write exactly like the original.
Coir	*n.*	the fibre of coconut husk.
Choir	*n.*	a company of singers or dancers.
Collision	*n.*	a clash.
Collusion	*n.*	a secret agreement.
Comfort	*v.*	to soothe, to console.
Comport	*v.*	to agree, to accord.
Command	*v.*	to order.
Commend	*v.*	to praise.
Comment	*n.*	a critical remark.
Concede	*v.*	to give away.
Conceit	*n.*	whim.

Concert	*n.*	a public performance of music.
Consult	*v.*	to take advice from.
Confirm	*v.*	to make sure.
Conform	*v.*	to make like.
Congeal	*v.*	to freeze.
Congenial	*adj.*	having same taste.
	adj.	pleasant.
Congenital	*adj.*	inborn.
Conscience	*n.*	the sense of right or wrong.
Conscious	*adj.*	aware of.
Conscientious	*adj.*	guided by conscience, careful.
Consensus	*n.*	general agreement.
Consonance	*n.*	agreement.
Consonant	*adj.*	a speech sound other than vowel.
Constant	*adj.*	firm.
Constituent	*adj.*	serving to compose.
Constitute	*v.*	to form.
Constrain	*v.*	to restrict or limit.
Constraint	*n.*	restriction.
Constrained	*adj.*	not natural.
Contact	*n.*	connection.
Contract	*n.*	written agreement.
Cataract	*n.*	eye disease.
	n.	a waterfall.
Contain	*v.*	to hold.
Content	*adj.*	satisfied.
	n.	an index of the books.
Contest	*v.*	compete with others.
Context	*n.*	speech or text.
	n.	a situation when sth happens.
Convection	*n.*	the conveying of heat from one part of a liquid to another.
Conviction	*n.*	the act of convicting.
	n.	a strong opinion or belief.

Convenience	*n.*	easy or quick to do.
Conveyance	*n.*	a vehicle.
	n.	the document by which property is conveyed.
Corporal	*adj.*	relating to the body.
	n.	a person of lower ranks in the army.
Corporeal	*adj.*	physical & not spiritual.
Crisis	*n.*	a moment of great danger.
Crises	*n.*	*plu.* of *crisis.*
Crush	*v.*	to break into pieces.
Curse	*n.*	an utterance of destruction.
Cub	*n.*	young ones of loin, tiger etc.
Cube	*n.*	a solid body having six equal sides.
Cue	*n.*	a signal for action.
	n.	a long stick used in Billiards, Pool & Snooker.
Queue	*n.*	a line of vehicles or people.
Custom	*n.*	habit, practice.
Customs	*n.*	tax, custom duty.
Costume	*n.*	clothes worn by actors in a play.
Dead	*adj.*	not alive.
	adj.	belonging to the past.
	adj.	not working.
	adj.	numb, insensitive.
	adv.	completely, very, extremely.
	n.	people who have died.
Died	*v.*	*p.t. & p.p.* of *die.*
Dearth	*n.*	a scarce supply.
Death	*n.*	the act of dying.
Decease	*n.*	death.
Disease	*n.*	ill health.
Decree	*n.*	an official order from a ruler.
	v.	to decide, to judge.
Decry	*v.*	condemn.
Deem	*v.*	to think.
Dim	*adj.*	faint.
Dime	*n.*	an American coin.

Defense or defence	*n.*	protection.
Defiance	*n.*	disobedience.
Definite	*adj.*	clear & distinct.
Definitive	*adj.*	decisive, unconditional.
Delicacy	*n.*	softness, choice kind of food.
Delicate	*adj.*	tender, fragile.
Dene	*n.*	a sandy tract.
Dean	*n.*	head of a faculty in the university.
Derive	*v.*	to take or develop from sth.
Drive	*v.*	*drove, driven.* to run a vehicle.
	v.	to force sb to act in a particular way.
	n.	an organized effort.
	n.	a part of computer.
Descend	*v.*	to go down.
Decent	*adj.*	becoming, modest.
Descent	*n.*	downward slope.
	n.	ancestary.
Dissent	*v.*	to differ in opinion.
Desist	*v.*	to stop doing sth.
Detract	*v.*	to diminish its value or merit.
Digest	*v.*	to digest food.
Distract	*v.*	to draw away attention.
Device	*n.*	tool.
Devise	*v.*	contrive, invent, to think up.
Devote	*v.*	to dedicate.
Devout	*adj.*	religious personage.
Devour	*v.*	to eat quickly.
	n.	a collection of short reports.
Did	*v.*	*do, did, done.*
Deed	*n.*	act, a legal signed document.
Diet	*n.*	food & drink.
Digit	*n.*	any of the figures from 0 to 9.
Dight	*v.*	to adorn.
Dilate	*v.*	to expand in all direction.
Dilute	*v.*	to mix liquid.

Dim	*adj.*	not bright.
	adj.	vague.
	adj.	not intelligent.
Deem	*v.*	consider.
Dime	*n.*	ten cents.
Dine	*v.*	to take dinner.
Din	*n.*	a loud noise.
Dint	*n.*	by means of sth
Displace	*v.*	to put sth out of usual place.
Display	*v.*	to show.
Distance	*n.*	amount of space between two places.
Distant	*adj.*	remote.
Dive	*v.*	to plunge into water.
Dives	*n.*	a rich & luxurious person.
Diverge	*v.*	to go in different direction.
Diverse	*adj.*	different.
Divorce	*n.*	the legal ending of marriage.
Do	*v.*	to execute, to perform.
	n.	a party, social event.
	abbre.	ditto.
Doe	*n.*	the female of yellow deer.
Due	*adj.*	owing, fit.
Dole	*n.*	money given by the government to unemployed people.
Doleful	*adj.*	very sad, mournful.
Doll	*n.*	a child's toy.
	n.	used for an attractive woman.
Don	*n.*	important personage.
Done	*p.p.*	of *do.*
Dun	*adj.*	of grayish brown.
	n.	importunate creditor.
Dune	*n.*	low sand hill on sea coast.
Doom	*n.*	death or destruction.
	v.	to make sth certain to fail, suffer.
Dome	*n.*	a round roof with a circular base.

Draft	*n.*	a sketch or rough copy.
	n.	a written orders for the payment of money.
Draught	*n.*	a flow of cool air in a room.
	n.	the amount of liquid swallowed.
Drought	*n.*	a large rainless period of time.
Drawn	*v.*	*draw, drew, drawn.* to make pictures, to pull, to withdraw.
	adj.	looking pale & thin.
Drone	*n.*	male honey bee.
	v.	to make low noise for a long time.
Drown	*v.*	to push & suffocate in water.
Dully	*adj.*	dull.
	adv.	in a dull manner.
Duly	*adv.*	properly, rightly.
Dwell	*v.*	to live in a certain place.
Dell	*n.*	deep valley, a hollow.
Egress	*n.*	a way out or an exit.
Ingress	*n.*	a place or means of entering.
Either	*conj.*	one of the two, both.
Ether	*n.*	highly flammable liquid.
Ether	*n.*	clear sky.
Elder	*adj.*	older.
Elder	*n.*	small tree with white flowers & black berries.
Alder	*n.*	tree related to the birch.
Elegy	*n.*	a poem of sorrow for the dead.
Eulogy	*n.*	high praise about sb.
Else	*adv.*	in addition or more.
Also	*adv.*	in addition, too.
Also ran	*n.*	loser in a race, competition or election.
Embar	*v.*	to shut in, to hinder.
Ember	*n.*	a piece of coal red after fire has died.
Umber	*n.*	a dark brown colour.
Emigrate	*v.*	to leave a country permanently & live in another one.
Immigrate	*v.*	to come & live permanently in a different country.

Migrate	*v.*	to move from one town, country etc. to go & live or work in another.
Émigré	*v.*	exile.
Empathy	*n.*	ability to imagine ourselves in that position.
Sympathy	*n.*	having fellow feeling for sb.
Epilogue	*n.*	a short speech at the end of a play.
Prologue	*n.*	a poem introducing a play, preface.
Erect	*adj.*	straight.
	v.	to build sth.
	v.	to put sth up.
Eruct	*v.*	to belch.
Arrect	*adj.*	alert, upright.
Errand	*n.*	business entrusted.
Errant	*adj.*	wandering in search of adventures.
Essence	*n.*	the most important quality of sth.
Incense	*n.*	fragrant gums & their odours.
	v.	make very angry.
Etcetera	*abbre.*	and other similar things.
Ex-creta	*n.*	faeces.
Ethic	*n.*	moral, principles.
Ethnic	*adj.*	connected to a nation, people, race.
	n.	a person from an ethnic minority.
Evasion	*n.*	avoidance.
Invasion	*n.*	invading.
Event	*n.*	anything which happens.
Invent	*v.*	to devise something new.
Evoke	*v.*	to call up.
Invoke	*v.*	to call on God for help.
Exalt	*v.*	to raise, to praise highly.
Exult	*v.*	to feel great joy or triumph.
Example	*n.*	illustration.
Exemplar	*n.*	model.
Exemplary	*adj.*	worthy of imitation.

Exception	*n.*	not included in a norm.
Exceptional	*adj.*	outstanding.
Exemption	*n.*	excuse from duty or payment.
Excite	*v.*	stimulate, arouse
Incite	*v.*	to encourage to do sth illegal.
Excuse	*n.*	explanation offered to justify a fault.
Accuse	*v.*	charge with wrong doing.
Exercise	*n.*	bodily exertion for developing health.
	v.	to use power, rights etc.
Exorcise	*v.*	to free a person of evil spirits.
Expatiate	*v.*	to write or speak in detail about a subject.
Expatriate	*n.*	who is not living in his own country.
Expert	*adj.*	skillful, a specialist.
Excerpt	*n.*	short piece of writing taken from a longer whole.
Exert	*v.*	to perform.
Extant	*adj.*	still standing or existing.
Extent	*n.*	how large, important, etc. sth is.
Extend	*v.*	to make sth longer & larger.
Extinct	*adj.*	no longer in existence or active.
Extract	*v.*	pull out by force, remove.
	n.	a passage.
Exact	*adj.*	precise, meticulous.
Abstract	*adj.*	a quality, idea or feeling rather than a material
	n.	object.
	n.	a type of painting.
	n.	a summary.
Fable	*n.*	a short story depicting animals as characters & teaching a lesson.
Foible	*n.*	a minor fault in sb's character.
Face	*n.*	front of head.
	v.	to confront, to be opposite.
	v.	to deal with difficult situation.
Faeces (also feces)	*n.*	excrement.
Facial	*adj.*	of the face.
Facile	*adj.*	easy.
Facilitate	*v.*	to make easy or easier.
Felicitate	*v.*	to wish joy or happiness to.

Facility	*n.*	sth provided for specific purpose.
Felicity	*n.*	great happiness.
Faction	*n.*	self interested political party.
Fraction	*n.*	small portion.
Factitious		artificially achieved.
Fictitious		invented.
Fail	*v.*	not to succeed.
Fell	*n.*	an animal's skin or hide.
Fell	*v.*	*fell, felled, felled. to cut down.*
Flail	*v.*	to beat or strike with a flail.
Faith	*n.*	trust, belief.
Faithful	*adj.*	loyal.
Faithfully	*adv.*	accurately, carefully.
Fallow	*adj.*	*(of land)* ploughed but left unplanted.
Fellow	*n.*	companion, comrade.
Famine	*n.*	lack of food during a long period of time.
Feminine	*adj.*	*(gender)* having female qualities.
Fanny	*n.*	the buttocks.
Funny	*adj.*	comical, strange.
Farce	*n.*	a funny play.
Force	*n.*	physical strength, power.
Farmer	*n.*	one who does farming.
Former	*adj.*	earlier, the first of the two.
Farther	*adj .& adv.*	additional more distant.
Father	*n.*	*opp* gender of mother.
Further	*adj.*	more remote, to a greater degree or extent.
Farrow	*v.*	to give birth to.
Furrow	*n.*	rage.
	n.	trench made by a plough.
Fashion	*n.*	style in clothes, hair etc popular at a particular time
Fission	*n.*	splitting.
Fusion	*n.*	melting.
Passion	*n.*	intense sexual love, any strong emotion.

Feast	*n.*	a large special meal.
Fist	*n.*	a hand with fingers tightly closed.
First	*adj.*	foremost in time or order.
Fertile	*adj.*	that produces good result.
Futile	*adj.*	useless.
Feud	*n.*	a quarrel.
Food	*n.*	things eaten.
Fiction	*n.*	literature having imaginary events.
Friction	*n.*	the force.
Faction	*n.*	minority group within a large body.
Fictional	*adj.*	imaginary.
Fictitious	*adj.*	invented or unreal, not genuine.
Functional	*adj.*	practical & useful, utilitarian.
Fiend	*n.*	an evil spirit, fanatic.
Find	*v.*	*found, found.* to discover by chance.
Figment	*n.*	sth imagined that does not exist.
Pigment	*n.*	colouring matter.
Final	*adj.*	last, decisive.
	n.	the end.
Finale	*n.*	the end, the termination of drama.
Finial	*n.*	a decorative part at the top of roof, wall etc.
Finally	*adv.*	eventually.
Finely	*adv.*	splendidly.
Fire	*n.*	the flames after burning.
	n.	shots from guns.
	n.	strong emotions, anger etc.
Pyre	*n.*	a large pile of wood for funeral ceremony.
Flaccid	*adj.*	soft & yielding.
Placid	*adj.*	calm, mild.
Flair	*n.*	talent.
Flare	*v.*	erupt.
	n.	bright but unsteady light.
Flam	*n.*	deception, falsehood.
Flame	*n.*	yellow sight after burning.
Phlegm	*n.*	the thick substance that forms in nose & throat.

Flour	*n.*	the finely ground meal of wheat.
Floor	*n.*	the bottom surface of a room.
Flower	*n.*	a blossom.
Flow	*v.*	*flew, flown.* to run as a liquid.
Follow	*v.*	to chase, to go or come after.
Forbade	*v.*	*forbid, forbade, forbidden.* to prevent.
Forebode	*v.*	to predict.
Form	*n.*	shape or appearance.
	n.	class in a school.
	n.	state of health.
	n.	paper with spaces to fill in.
	v.	to shape, to construct, to develop.
Forum	*n.*	a place where people exchange opinions.
From	*prep.*	to show source, out of, away.
Fro	*adv.*	from, away, backward.
Forth	*adv.*	towards, out or away.
Fourth	*adj.*	number four in series.
	n.	a quarter.
Froth	*n.*	foam.
Fragment	*n.*	small part of sth.
Fragrant	*adj.*	having pleasant smell.
Fry	*n.*	young fish just spawned.
	v.	process of cooking.
Fray	*n.*	a brawl, a contest.
Gain	*v.*	to acquire.
Gainly	*adv.*	gracefully, pleasing.
Gainful	*adj.*	useful.
Gale	*n.*	a violent wind.
	n.	a shrub found in marshes.
Gall	*n.*	blister, sore, impudent, resentment.
	n.	bile.
	n.	oak apple.
Gal	*n.*	a girl or woman.
Gala	*n.*	a special public celebration.
Gambit	*n.*	an action intended to gain an advantage.
Gamut	*n.*	the entire range or extents.

Gamble	*v.*	to play for money, to bet.
Gambol	*n.*	a skipping about, a frolic.
Gander	*n.*	male goose, quick look.
Gender	*n.*	state of being male or female.
Gap	*n.*	an opening, space between two things.
Gape	*v.*	to be wide open, to stare at.
Gargle	*v.*	wash the throat with a liquid.
Gurgle	*v.*	to make a bubbling noise.
Gas	*n.*	any substance like air.
	v.	to chat.
Gash	*n.*	a long deep cut.
Guess	*v.*	to speculate.
Gazelle	*n.*	a small antelope.
Guzzle	*v.*	to drink sth in large amounts.
Gem	*n.*	precious stone.
Germ	*n.*	the rudiment of animal or plant.
Gene	*n.*	a chromosome.
Jean	*n.*	fabric.
German	*adj. & n.*	a native or language of Germany.
German	*adj.*	closely related.
Germane	*adj.*	appropriate, relevant.
Germen	*n.*	seed vessel, ovary.
Glad	*adj.*	pleased & happy.
Glade	*n.*	open space in forest.
Glass	*n.*	a hard transparent material.
Glasses	*n.*	*plu.* spectacles.
Glen	*n.*	deep narrow valley.
Glean	*v.*	gather facts etc. bit by bit.
Goad	*n.*	a sharp pointed stick to drive cattle.
	v.	to keep irritating.
God	*n.*	the Providence.
Got	*p.t.*	of *get.*
Goat	*n.*	a horned four footed animal.
Gout	*n.*	a disease of joints.

Grainy	*adj.*	full of grains.
Granny	*n.*	grand mother, an old woman.
Gram	*n.*	chick pea. *(chana).*
	n.	the unit of weight in metric system.
Grama	*n.*	a kind of low grass.
Grate	*n.*	framework of iron bars.
Grateful	*adj.*	thankful.
Great	*adj.*	large, eminent.
Greet	*v.*	to salute, to welcome.
Grave	*n.*	a burial place for dead.
	n.	accent over a vowel to indicate special pronunciation.
	adj.	serious, important.
Grab	*v.*	seize
Groove	*n.*	a furrow or long hollow.
Grove	*n.*	a group of trees.
Gut	*n.*	intestine, belly.
	v.	to destroy the inside or contents of a building.
	adj.	based on feelings & emotions.
Guts	*n.*	the courage & determination.
Habit	*n.*	custom, practice, tendency.
Habitat	*n.*	the natural home of an animal or plant.
Habitable	*n.*	fit to live in.
Hack	*v.*	to cut sth with blow.
	n.	sb who does work that is not important or original.
	n.	a horse for ordinary riding.
Hake	*n.*	a sea fish of the cod family.
Had	*p.t. & p.p.* of *have.*	
Hades	*n.*	the underworld.
Head	*n.*	the upper part of body.
	adj.	chief.
	v.	to lead.
Hail	*n.*	frozen drops of rain.
Hail	*interj.*	Bravo.
	v.	to call sb in order to say hello.
Hale	*adj.*	healthy, sound.

Hair	*n.*	thread like fiber on skin.
Hare	*n.*	timid rodent like rabbit.
Hear	*v.*	to listen.
Heir	*n.*	successor.
Here	*adv.*	in or at this place, at this point.
Hire	*n.*	money paid for work done.
Halo	*n.*	luminous circle round the sun or moon, nimbus.
Hallo, hello	*interj.*	to greet.
Hallow	*n.*	a holy person or saint.
	v.	to execute, to chase with shouts.
Hollow	*adj.*	having a cavity, empty.
Halt	*v.*	to stop.
Holt	*n.*	a wood, an orchard.
Hamlet	*n.*	a small village.
Helmet	*n.*	a head protection.
Hamper	*n.*	a large covered basket.
Hamper	*n.*	shackles.
	v.	to hinder , to impede.
Handicap	*n.*	disability.
Hand cuff	*n.*	a pair of metal rings to be put on the wrists of prisoners.
Handsome	*adj.*	pleasing & dignified in form or appearance.
Hansom	*n.*	a two wheeled horse drawn carriage.
Happen	*v.*	to occur.
Hyphen	*n.*	(-) a mark of punctuation.
Hard	*adj.*	solid, difficult, tough.
Hardly	*adv.*	almost not, scarcely.
Has	*singu.*	of *have.*
Hash	*v.*	to chop.
	n.	the symbol-(#).
Haze	*n.*	mist, vapour.
Hat	*n.*	a covering to fit the head.
Hate	*v.*	to dislike.
	n.	hatred.

Hatch	*n.*	a lower half door.
	v.	to hatch eggs.
Have	*v.*	own, hold, consist of, possess
	aux., v.	used with *p.p.* to form perfect tense.
Have to	*modal.*	used to show that the work is done due to some boundation.
Haves	*v.*	people having wealth.
Halve	*v.*	to reduce by a half.
Heal	*v.*	to restore to health, to make well.
Hell	*n.*	*opp* of *heaven.*
Heel	*n.*	back part of the foot below the ankle.
	n.	unpleasant man.
Hill	*n.*	a small mountain.
Hearth	*n.*	floor of fire place.
Heath	*n.*	waste land, moor.
Health	*n.*	the condition of person's body.
Heat	*n.*	hotness.
	v.	to make hot.
Height	*n.*	altitude.
Hit	*v.*	to strike with a blow.
	n.	a person or thing that is very popular.
Heed	*v.*	to pay attention to.
Hid	*v.*	*hide, hid, hidden.*
Herd	*n.*	a flock of animals of one kind.
Heard	*v.*	*p.t. & p.p.* of *hear.*
Heroin	*n.*	a drug.
Heroine	*n.*	a female hero.
Heron	*n.*	long legged wading bird.
Hey	*expression.*	shout.
Hie	*v.*	to go quickly.
Hi	*excl.*	to say hello.
High	*n.*	an elevated place.
	adj.	towering.
	adv.	far up.
Historian	*n.*	writer of history.
Histrian	*n.*	a stage player.

Hoard	*n.*	stock, store.
	v.	to lay up.
Horde	*n.*	a tribe of nomads, a troop.
Hoarse	*adj.*	rough & harsh sounding.
Horse	*n.*	four footed animal used for riding.
Hole	*n.*	a hollow.
Whole	*adj.*	healthy, entire.
	n.	sum.
Holey	*n.*	full of holes.
Holly	*n.*	bushes.
Holy	*adj.*	Godly, divine.
Holm	*n.*	rich land by river.
Home	*n.*	one's fixed residence.
Homonym	*n.*	a word that is spelt like another word but has a different meaning.
Homophone	*n.*	a word that is pronounced like another word but has a different meaning.
Honourable	*adj.*	deserving respect.
Honorarium	*n.*	payment made for sb's professional services.
Honorary	*adj.*	given as an honour without getting the actual qualification.
Hoof	*n.*	the horny substance on an animal's foot.
Hoop	*v.*	to make a wheezy sound.
	n.	a large ring of plastic, wood or iron.
Hose	*n.*	flexible pipe for conveying liquids.
	n.	stockings, socks & tights.
House	*n.*	building used as home.
Hospital	*n.*	an institution for the cure of the sick.
Hospitality	*n.*	generous reception of guests.
Hostel	*n.*	living house for students.
Hostile	*adj.*	opposed, adverse.
Hue	*n.*	colour, shade.
Hew	*v.*	*hewed, hewed.* cut with an axe.

Hug	*v.*	to embrace.
	n.	a close embrace.
Huge	*adj.*	of great size.
Human	*adj.*	belonging to human beings.
Humane	*adj.*	kind, benevolent.
Humerus	*n.*	*pl. humeri.* the large bone in the top part of the arm
	n.	between the shoulder & elbow.
Humorous	*adj.*	funny & entertaining.
Hydra	*n.*	a water serpent with many heads.
Hydro	*pref.*	in the sense of water.
Hymen	*n.*	the God of marriage.
Hymn	*n.*	sacred song in praise.
Him	*pron.*	*objective case* of *he.*
Hyperbole	*n.*	a figures of speech *(exaggeration).*
Hyperbola	*n.*	a term in geometry.
Imitate	*v.*	to copy.
Intimate	*adj.*	close.
Intimidate	*v.*	to make sb afraid or insecure.
Immoral	*adj.*	not moral.
Amoral	*adj.*	ignorant of morality.
Immortal	*adj., n.*	having eternal life or existence.
Impassable	*adj.*	unable to overcome.
Impassible	*adj.*	being incapable of feelings.
Impossible	*adj.*	incapable of happening.
Important	*adj.*	of great value.
Impotent	*adj.*	powerless in sex *(of man).*
Impostor	*n.*	a pretender of false identity.
Imposture	*n.*	deception by fraudulent impersonation.
Impoverish	*v.*	to make poor.
Improvise	*v.*	to make sth using whatever is available.
Imprudent	*adj.*	unwise or indiscreet.
Impudent	*adj.*	showing a lack of respect.
Inane	*adj.*	very silly & stupid.
Insane	*adj.*	mentally ill.

Industrial	*adj.*	connected with industry.
Industrious	*adj.*	hard working.
Infer	*v.*	work out from evidence.
Infra	*pref.*	below or beyond a particular limit.
Inmate	*n.*	person living in an institution such as a prison or hospital.
Innate	*adj.*	natural, inborn.
Intense	*adj.*	of great strength or degree.
Intent	*n.*	intention.
Inter	*v.*	to bury a dead person.
	pref.	between, from one to another.
Enter	*v*	to come or go into sth.
	v.	to join institution.
Intra	*pref.*	inside, within.
Interest	*n.*	wanting to know more.
	n.	hobby.
	n.	the extra money paid back on the borrowed money.
Interested	*adj.*	showing interest in sth.
Interesting	*adj.*	exciting or unusual.
Institution	*n.*	an important organization that has a particular purpose.
Intuition	*n.*	the ability to know sth by using the feelings.
Iron	*n.*	hard strong metal.
	v.	to press clothes.
	v.	to get rid of any problem.
	adj.	very strong, determined.
Ironic	*adj.*	show the opposite meaning of what is said.
Irony	*n.*	a situation different from what is expected.
Keen	*adj.*	having a sharp edge.
	v.	to lament for dead.
Ken	*n.*	range of sight or knowledge.
Kin	*n.*	race, family.
Kiln	*n.*	a large oven for backing bricks.

Kindle	*v.*	to start burning.
Kindling	*n.*	small dry pieces of wood.
Kindly	*adv.*	in a kind way.
Label	*n.*	tag, ticket.
Labial	*n.*	a speech sound made with lips.
Level	*n.*	a particular standard or quality.
	adj.	flat, equal.
	v.	to raze.
Liable	*adj.*	legally bound, answerable, prone.
Libel	*n.*	printing a false statement about sb.
Labour	*n.*	exertion of the body or mind.
	n.	childbirth.
	v.	to struggle or do hard work.
Labor	*n.*	labour.
Labourer	*n.*	a worker.
Lamp	*n.*	a device that produces light.
Lump	*n.*	a piece of sth hard or solid.
Land	*n.*	the dry part of earth.
	v.	to come down to the ground.
	v.	to take off.
Lend	*v.*	*lent, lent.* to let out on hire, loan.
Lawyer	*n.*	advocate.
Liar	*n.*	who tells lie.
Linear	*adj.*	of a line or lines, of length.
Liner	*n.*	a passenger ship.
Literator	*n.*	a literary man.
Literature	*n.*	of books & writings.
Lose	*v.*	to be deprived of.
Loss	*n.*	act of losing.
Lure	*v.*	entice.
Lore	*n.*	tales told by a particular group of people.
Lores	*adj.*	low resolution.
Lust	*n.*	very strong sexual desire.
Lusture	*n*	the brightness, sheen.
Lusty	*adj.*	healthy & strong.

Luxurious	*adj.*	comfortable having expensive things.
Luxuriant	*adj.*	rich & attractive.
Manual	*adj.*	work done with hands.
Menial	*adj.*	low paid work.
Marital	*adj.*	related to marriage.
Martial	*adj.*	of war, warlike.
Marrow	*n.*	the bone marrow.
Morrow	*n.*	the next day, tomorrow.
Mar	*v.*	to spoil, to ruin.
Mars	*n.*	the God of war.
	n.	a red planet.
Marsh	*n.*	a swamp.
Mask	*n.*	covering to hide or protect face.
	v.	to disguise.
Masque	*n.*	a play written in verse.
Mosque	*n.*	Muslim worship place.
Master	*n.*	person in control.
	adj.	over all or controlling.
	v.	to get knowledge & skill in, overcome.
Muster	*v.*	assemble, gather.
Mastery	*n.*	command or knowledge of sth.
Mystery	*n.*	that is difficult to understand or explain.
May	*modal aux.*,	expressing possibility, permission, wish, pray etc.
	n.	the fifth month of the year.
My	*poss.*	*adj.* (I).
Meander	*v.*	wander, to curve.
Mender	*n.*	a person who mends sth.
Minder	*n.*	one who takes care of another.
Medal	*v.*	a metal piece given as a prize.
Meddle	*v.*	to interfere.
Medial	*adj.*	average.
Middle	*adj.*	intermediate.
	n.	the centre of any thing.

Mentor	*n.*	*guru.*
Monitor	*n.*	head boy in the class.
	v.	to supervise.
	n.	a television or computer screen.
Mercenary	*n.*	a soldier who fights for the party who pays him.
	adj.	money minded.
Missionary	*n.*	who takes job as a mission.
Metal	*n.*	a solid mineral substance.
Mettle	*n.*	ability & determination.
Meteor	*n.*	a shooting star.
Métier	*n.*	one's profession or job.
Mind	*n.*	intellect, brain.
	v.	to look after.
	v.	to feel upset or annoyed.
Mend	*v.*	to repair.
Minute	*n.*	sixty seconds.
	adj.	precise, tiny, very small.
	n.	record of decisions taken in a meeting.
	n.	we measure angles in minutes.
Minuet	*n.*	a piece of music.
Minutiae	*n.*	very small details.
Missal	*n.*	a book containing prayers etc.
Missel	*n.*	mistle thrush.
Missile	*n.*	a fighting weapon that explodes.
Missive	*n.*	letter.
Massive	*adj.*	large & heavy.
Mixer	*n.*	an instrument which mixes.
Mixture	*n.*	the act of mixing.
Moment	*n.*	a short period of time.
Memento	*n.*	souvenir.
Movement	*n.*	a group of people working for an aim.
	n.	changing position.

Most	*det., pron.* the largest number or amount.	
	s*uperlative* of much, a lot of, many.	
	adv.	to the greatest degree.
	suff.	the furthest.
Moist	*adj.*	damp.
Mote	*n.*	a spec of dust.
Moat	*n.*	water filled ditch around a castle.
Motte	*n.*	a castle mound.
Motel	*n.*	a hotel with car parking facility.
Hotel	*n.*	a building for stay of people where they pay for the facilities provided.
Motif	*n.*	design or pattern to decorate.
Motive	*n.*	intent.
Mound	*n.*	an artificial elevation of the earth.
Mount	*n.*	a mountain, hill.
	v.	to climb, to increase.
Muslim	*n.*	believer in the religion of Islam.
Muslin	*n.*	fine cotton fabric.
Natural	*adj.*	inborn, relating to nature.
Neutral	*adj.*	impartial, unbiased.
Naturalism	*n.*	to depict life as real.
Naturism	*n.*	aesthetic sense towards nature's beauty.
Nature	*n.*	all the creation on the earth.
	n.	main features of sth.
	n.	real character of sb.
Neuter	*adj.*	one of the types of Gender Nurture
	n. & v.	education, fostering.
Nil	*n.*	nothing.
Kneel	*v.*	to bow on knees.
Knell	*n.*	the stroke of bell rung at a funeral.
Nill	*v.*	not to like.
Nose	*n.*	an organ of body which smells.
Noose	*n.*	a snare.

Not	*adv.*	used to form negative.
Note	*n.*	a short piece of writing as reminder.
	n.	a piece of paper money.
	n.	a single sound of a particular length & pitch *(music).*
	v.	jot down.
Knot	*n.*	a join made by two pieces of strings.
	n.	a way of twisting hair.
	n.	a hard round spot in piece of wood.
	n.	a tight hard feeling in stomach, throat etc.
	n.	unit for measuring speed of boat & aircraft.
	v.	to fasten with knot.
Naught, Nought	*n.*	nothing.
Notion	*n.*	an idea.
Nation	*n.*	a country, population.
Now	*adv.*	at the present moment.
Know	*v.*	to be aware of.
Obese	*adj.*	very fat.
Obsess	*v.*	to think about a particular thing all the while.
Observe	*v.*	to see, to celebrate.
Absorb	*v.*	to swallow up.
Absolve	*v.*	to set free.
Obsolete	*adj.*	out of use.
Absolute	*adj.*	independent, sole.
Occident	*n.*	the western part of the world.
Accident	*n.*	incident that happens by chance.
Oft	*adv.*	often.
Opt	*v.*	to choose, to take.
One's	*det.*	*poss.* of *one.*
Once	*adj.*	on one occasion only, at some time in the past.
Ounce	*n.*	unit of weight.
Opine	*v.*	to think, to express opinion.
Opinion	*n.*	view, notion, belief.
Overdo	*v.*	to do excess.
Overdue	*adj.*	still due after the time allowed.

Pageant	*n.*	any brilliant show.
Peasant	*n.*	a cultivator, a rustic.
Pheasant	*n.*	a game bird.
Pageantry	*n.*	events of brilliant show.
Peasantry	*n.*	all the peasants in a region.
Parity	*n.*	the state of being equal.
Party	*n.*	a group of people doing sth together.
Park	*n.*	an area of public land.
	v.	to park vehicle.
Perk	*n.*	sth received for doing a job.
Parson	*n.*	parish priest in the Church of England.
Person	*n.*	human being.
		Grammar. three persons of pronoun.
Persona	*n.*	sb's personality as shown.
Past	*adj & n.*	gone by, ended, one of the three Tenses.
Paste	*n.*	kneaded flour.
Pest	*n.*	harmful thing or person.
Pasture	*n.*	a grass land.
Posture	*n.*	physical or mental attitude.
Patient	*adj.*	showing patience.
	n.	a sick person in the hospital.
Patent	*n.*	the right to sell & make use of some invention.
Pause	*v.*	to stop for some time.
Pose	*v.*	to create a threat, problem etc.
	v.	to give a position for photograph.
	n.	affectation.
Posh	*adj.*	elegant & expensive, stylish.
Peace	*n.*	calm.
Pease	*n.*	peas collectively.
Piece	*n.*	a fragment, a portion.
Pice	*n.*	a coin.
Pious	*adj.*	devout, religious, holy.
People	*n.*	persons, men, women, children.
Pupil	*n.*	a taught, student.

Perfect	*adj.*	faultless, complete.
Prefect	*n.*	a head boy or girl in an institution.
Personal	*adj.*	of a person.
Personnel	*n.*	the employees of any organization.
Persuade	*v.*	to convince.
Pursued	*v.*	to follow.
Physic	*n.*	medical art or science.
Physique	*n.*	bodily structure & development.
Physics	*n.*	a branch of study, a science subject.
Pistil	*n.*	part of a flower containing seeds.
Pistol	*n.*	short barreled gun.
Place	*n.*	position, point or area.
Palace	*n.*	building where king lives.
Plaice	*n.*	flat sea fish.
Placenta	*n.*	afterbirth.
Pleasant	*adj.*	enjoyable, attractive, friendly.
Planet	*n.*	a celestial body revolving round the sun.
Planent	*adj.*	thrilling, loud & mournful.
Plant	*n.*	a living thing growing in the earth having stem, leaves & roots.
	n.	a factory, machinery.
	v.	to put sth strongly in a place.
	v.	to plant tree.
Plaint	*n.*	accusation, lamentation.
Ply	*v.*	to work at steadily.
Play	*v.*	to take part in game.
	n.	a drama.
Poll	*n.*	process of election.
	n.	the head.
Pole	*n.*	a long stick set straight in the ground.
	n.	north or south poles.
Pool	*n.*	a small still water area.
	n.	a game played by two.
	v.	to gather sth.

Pond	*n.*	a small body of still water.
Pound	*v.*	to make into powder.
	n.	an enclosure for stray cattle.
	n.	a measure of weight.
Portable	*adj.*	that is easy to carry or to move.
Potable	*adj.*	safe to drink *(water).*
Pose	*v.*	to create a threat, problem.
	v.	to give position for getting photographed.
Posh	*adj.*	elegant & expensive.
Paws	*n.*	the feet of an animal.
Poise	*n.*	calm & confident manner.
Precede	*v.*	to go before.
Proceed	*v.*	to continue as planned.
Précis	*n.*	an abstract or summary.
Precise	*adj.*	exact, definite, distinct.
	adj.	meticulous.
Pre pone	*v.*	to move sth to an earlier time than scheduled.
Postpone	*v.*	to put off.
Preposition	*n.*	a word that shows the relation between two words.
Proposition	*n.*	a proposal, an assertion.
Prescribe	*v.*	to order to do sth.
Proscribe	*v.*	to order not to do sth.
Price	*n.*	the amount paid as cost of sth.
Prize	*n.*	a reward.
	adj.	treasure.
Prise	*v.*	to use force to separate sth from sth else.
Praise	*n., v.*	complement, admire.
Private	*adj.*	personal, not public.
Privet	*n.*	an ornamental shrub used in hedges.
Property	*n.*	possessions including land or building.
Propriety	*n.*	correct conduct.
Protect	*v.*	to defend, to guard.
Protract	*v.*	to prolong.

Purl in	*n.*	horizontal beam in a roof.
Purloin	*v.*	to steal.
Purpose	*n.*	aim, intention.
Propose	*v.*	to make proposal.
Pyre	*n.*	pile of wood for burning a corpse.
Fire	*n.*	burning of fuel, flame.
Quiet	*adj.*	calm, still.
Quite	*adv.*	entirely, altogether.
Quit	*v.*	to abandon, to stop doing sth.
Rag	*n.*	torn cloth.
	v.	to tease.
Rage	*n.*	feeling of violent anger.
Ragged	*adj.*	old & torn, shabby.
	adj.	very tired.
Rugged	*adj.*	not level or smooth.
Raging	*adj.*	very strong.
Ragging	*v.*	to play trick on sb.
Rigging	*n.*	the ropes supporting the masts & sails of ship.
Raise	*v.*	to move upward.
Rise	*v.*	sth rises by itself.
Randem	*n.*	a carriage drawn by three horses.
Random	*adj.*	aimless, haphazard.
Rant	*v.*	to boast.
Rent	*n.*	amount paid for use of land, room etc.
	n.	a tear or hole in a material.
Rare	*adj.*	not dense, unusual, uncommon.
Rear	*n.*	the hind most part.
	v.	to raise, to build, to breed, to educate.
Real	*adj.*	true, actually.
Reel	*n.*	a dance, a bobbin.
	n.	to move in a very unsteady way.
	n.	a reel together with the film.
	v.	stagger.

Red	*adj.*	crimson.
Rad	*adj.*	very good.
	n.	a unit for measuring the effects of Radiation.
Raid	*n.*	sudden attack.
Read	*v.*	*p.t. & p.p.* of *read.*
Regal	*adj.*	royal, splendid.
Regale	*n.*	a feast.
Regrate	*v.*	to buy & sell in the same market due to which prices rise up.
Regret	*v.*	to repent.
Re greet	*v.*	to greet or salute again.
Relay	*n.*	relay race.
	v.	to broadcast a programme.
Rely	*v.*	to trust in.
Relieve	*v.*	to release from duty.
Relive	*v.*	to live again.
Remainder	*n.*	the rest.
Reminder	*n.*	send for reminding.
Repeal	*v.*	cancel.
Repel	*v.*	drive back, resist.
Reside	*v.*	dwell permanently.
Residue	*n.*	what is left, remainder.
Revel	*v.*	make merry.
Rebel	*n.*	mutineer.
Reveal	*v.*	to disclose, to display.
Rich	*adj.*	wealthy, fertile, splendid.
Riches	*n.*	wealth, opulence.
Reach	*v.*	to arrive, achieve aim.
	n.	the distance covered.
Rile	*v.*	to excite, to make angry.
Rill	*n.*	a small brook.
Relle	*n.*	a narrow furrow on the moon.
Rip	*v.*	to cut, to tear, to rush along.
Ripe	*adj.*	ready for reaping.
Reap	*v.*	harvest, to obtain sth.

Roam	*v.*	to wander.
Room	*n.*	a chamber to live in.
	v.	to rent a room somewhere.
Roaster	*n.*	one that roasts.
Roister	*v.*	make merry noisily.
Rooster	*n.*	the domestic cock.
Roster	*n.*	a list of duties turn wise.
Rose	*v.*	*rise, rose, risen.* to stand up.
	n.	a beautiful flower.
	adj.	pink in colour.
Ross	*n.*	the bark of a tree.
Sacred	*adj.*	holy, religious.
Secrete	*v.*	to produce fluids.
Secret	*adj.*	hidden, secluded
Sad	*adj.*	sorrowful.
Said	*v.*	*p.t. & p.p.* of *say.*
Sag	*v.*	to sink under pressure.
Saga	*n.*	long story.
Sage	*n.*	an aromatic herb used in cooking.
	n.	a wise person.
Sample	*n.*	specimen.
Simple	*adj.*	easy to understand or do.
Sand	*n.*	a substance found at sea shore.
Send	*v.*	*sent, sent.* to make sb go from one place to another.
Sans	*prep.*	without.
	adv.	until now.
Sansa	*n.*	thumb piano.
Sense	*n.*	one of the five powers *(sight, hearing, smell, taste & touch).*
	n.	normal state of mind.
	n.	meaning.
	v.	to feel, to guess.
	v.	become aware
Since	*prep.*	from a time. used for point of time as For is used for period of time.

Scar	*n.*	mark of a wound.
Scare	*v.*	to be afraid.
Scarce	*adj.*	available in small quantity.
	adv.	only just, almost not.
Scarcely	*adv.*	hardly.

Sensible	*adj.*	having good sense.
Sensitive	*adj.*	tender, emotional.

Sentence	*n.*	a group of meaningful words that makes a complete sense.
	n.	the punishment ordered by a court.
Sentience	*n.*	feeling, consciousness.

Sex	*n.*	character of being male or female, sexual activity. *combining form.*
Six	*number.*	five plus one.

Shot	*v.*	*shoot, shot, shot.* to fire gun.
Shout	*v.*	to say loudly.
	n.	a loud cry.

Size	*n.*	extant, volume, dimension.
Seize	*v.*	to put in possession.
Cease	*v.*	to stop.

Spec	*n.*	speculation.
Speck	*n.*	a small spot.
Specs	*n.*	pair of spectacles.
Spick	*adj.*	neat & clean.
Spike	*n.*	a thin object with a sharp point.

Species	*n.*	species of animals, plants etc.
Spices	*n.*	substance made from plants used in cooking.

Sceptre, scepter	*n.*	a royal power symbol.
Spectre, specter	*n.*	ghost.

Spell	*n.*	charm, fascination.
	v.	to tell the spelling of word.
	n.	period.
Spill	*v.*	*spilled, spilled* or *spilt, spilt. (of liquid)* to flow over a container.

Spilt	*v.*	*spill, spilled, spilled* also *spilt, spilt.* to overflow, to throw.
Split	*v.*	*split, split.* to cut into pieces, to divide.
Sport	*n.*	game, amusement.
Spot	*n.*	a mark, a blot.
Stag	*n.*	the male red deer.
Stage	*n.*	platform.
Stakeholder	*n.*	a person or group involved in an organization because they have invested money in it.
Stock holder	*n.*	a person who holds a stock.
Stick	*n.*	a rod, a staff.
Stick	*v.*	to stab, to adhere.
Strict	*adj.*	harsh.
Strife	*n.*	conflict.
Strive	*v.*	*strove, striven* (also) *strived, strived.* to struggle.
Submit	*v.*	to present for consideration, to urge.
Summit	*n.*	the top, the highest point.
Sub title	*n.*	second title of a book.
Subtle	*adj.*	not very noticeable or obvious.
Suc	*pref.*	in the sense of sub.
Suck	*v.*	to draw with mouth, to inhale.
Success	*n.*	act of succeeding.
Succession	*n.*	a series following on another.
Successor	*n.*	heir.
Super	*pref.*	in the sense of above beyond.
	adj.	excellent.
	n.	a supernumerary.
	adj.	capable of being overcome.
Supper	*n.*	the last meal of the day.
Surely	*adv.*	certainly.
Surly	*adj.*	rude, ill natured.
Swat	*n.*	a flexible bat for killing flies.
Swath	*n.*	a line of grass or grain cut.
Swathe	*n.*	bandage, a fold.

Sweat	*n.*	perspiration.
Sweet	*adj.*	sugary, melodious.
Swing	*v.*	to move to & fro.
	v.	change mood.
	n.	a seat for swinging on.
Swinge	*v.*	to beat soundly.
Taste	*n.*	liking, choice.
	v.	to detect the flavour by taste.
Test	*n.*	witness.
	n.	an examination.
	v.	to attest & date
	v.	to make a will.
	n.	trial.
Text	*n.*	written words.
Temple	*n.*	a building where Hindu worship.
	n.	the space between the forehead & the ear.
Trample	*v.*	to tread.
Tenant	*n.*	an occupant.
Tenet	*n.*	any opinion or principle.
Tenor	*n.*	a prevailing course or direction.
Tenure	*n.*	period of performing a task, duty.
Thirst	*n.*	desire for drink.
Thrust	*n.*	a push.
Thither	*adv.*	to that place.
Tether	*n.*	tie a beast with a rope or chain.
Thread	*n.*	any thin cord.
Threat	*n.*	menace.
Thumb	*n.*	the thick finger of human hand.
Thump	*v.*	to strike with heavy blow.
Tide	*n.*	rise & fall of sea.
	v.	to help sb in difficulty.
Tidings	*n.*	news.
Tied	*v.*	*p.t. & p.p.* of *tie.*
Tidy	*adj.*	arranged neatly & orderly.
	adj.	considerable amount.
	v.	to make sth look neat.
	n.	container for putting small objects.

Ting	*v.*	to tinkle.
Tinge	*n.*	faint colour.
Tinkle	*n.*	a light high ringing sound.
Twinkle	*v.*	twinkling of light.
Tinny	*adj.*	like tin.
Tiny	*adj.*	very small, minute.
Tomb	*n.*	grave.
Tome	*n.*	a large book.
Travel	*v.*	make a journey.
Travels	*n.*	account of journey.
Travail	*n.*	difficulties, sufferings.
Traverse	*v.*	to move from one area to another.
Trek	*v.*	to travel far on foot.
Track		a way, a railway line.
Tract	*n.*	region of indefinite extent.
Trail	*v.*	to draw along behind, to hunt.
	n.	a route followed for a particular purpose.
Trial	*n.*	judicial examination, test.
Trip	*n.*	a journey.
	v.	to fall or almost fall.
	v.	to release a switch etc.
Tripe	*n.*	garbage, rubbish.
Twin	*n.*	two born at a time.
Twine	*n.*	a strong twisted thread.
Union	*n.*	an association.
Unison	*n.*	done at the same time.
Unless	*conj.*	if not.
Unlace	*v.*	to undo the laces of shoes.
Unleash	*v.*	to suddenly let a strong force, emotion etc be felt.
Urban	*adj.*	living in a city or town.
Urbane	*adj.*	civil, polite.
Vacant	*adj.*	not occupied.
Vacate	*v.*	to leave place or post vacant.

Vassal	*n.*	a feudal tenant.
Vessel	*n.*	a utensil, container.
	n.	a ship or boat.
Verse	*n.*	poetry.
Versed	*adj.*	skilled, experienced.
Versus	*prep.*	against.
Vest	*n.*	a waist coat.
	v.	to belong to sb/sth legally.
Best	*n.*	*superlative* of *good.*
Vet	*n.*	veterinary surgeon.
	v.	to screen.
Bet	*v.*	to risk money by predicting the result.
Vetch	*n.*	a plant of pea family.
Vex	*v.*	frustrate, annoy.
Wax	*n.*	substance by which candle is made.
Vial	*n.*	phial.
Vile	*adj.*	disgusting.
Vis-à-vis	*prep.*	in relation to, in comparison with.
Viz	*adv.*	namely, that is.
Voice	*n.*	sound uttered by mouth.
Vice	*n.*	a fault, a defect.
Wag	*n.*	a moving to & fro.
	v.	to shake tail, finger.
	n.	joker.
Wage	*n.*	payment of work done, hire.
Wages	*n.*	to begin & continue war, a battle.
Vague	*adj.*	unclear.
Waive	*v.*	to put off.
Wave	*n.*	movement in the sea water.
	v.	to move hand in the air.
Weave	*v.*	to make cloth, carpet, basket etc by crossing threads.
Wander	*v.*	to roam aimlessly, to stray.
Wonder	*n.*	astonishment.

Want	*v.*	to have a desire or wish, need.
	n.	lack, being poor.
Wanton	*adj.*	causing harm deliberately.
Warm	*adj.*	temperately hot, wealthy.
Worm	*n.*	a small creeping animal.
Was	*p.t.*	first & third person singular of the verb be.
Wase	*n.*	wisp.
Wash	*v.*	to make clean using water.
Wearied	*adj.*	tired, exhausted.
Worried	*v.*	troubled.
Weary	*adj.*	very tired.
Worry	*v.*	to think about a problem.
Burry	*v.*	to place a dead body in a grave.
Well	*adv.*	in a good, right or acceptable way.
	adj.	in good health.
	excl.	used to express surprise, anger or relief.
	n.	deep hole in ground to obtain water.
We'll		*short form* we will, we shall.
What	*pron, det,* used in question.	
Watt	*n.*	a unit for measuring electrical power.
Wheen	*n.*	a small number of quantity.
When	*adv. & conj.* at what time.	
Whence	*adv.*	from where, from which.
While	*conj.*	when.
	n.	a period of time.
	v.	to spend time in a pleasant, lazy way.
Wile	*n.*	clever trick.
Whit	*n.*	a very small amount, jot.
Wit	*n.*	an ability to say or write cleverly.
Why	*adv.*	for what reason, because of which.
Whey	*n.*	the watery part of curd milk.
Wicked	*adj.*	roguish, depraved.
Wicket	*n.*	a small gate, *(cricket)* three fixed stumps for bowling at.

Wield	*v.*	to manage, to handle, to control.
Wild	*adj.*	uncivilized, which live in forest.
Weld	*v.*	to hammer into union.
	n.	a plant affording a yellow.
Wife	*n.*	*opp* of *husband.*
Wipe	*v.*	to erase.
Wive	*v.*	to marry, to take as wife.
Wight	*n.*	a person, a creature.
White	*adj.*	*opp* of *black.*
Win	*v.*	to gain victory.
Bin	*n.*	a container to put waste in.
	v.	to throw sth away.
Wind	*v.*	*p.t. & p.p. wound.* to turn, to coil.
	v.	to turn a handle several times.
	n.	air.
Worth	*adj.*	having a value in money etc.
Worthy	*adj.*	deserving.

4

CONFUSION IN USAGE

A/An/The

These are known as Articles in English Grammar.

A—*indefinite article.* one, each, any one, per. Used before consonant sounds. As — a boy, a car, a mango, a university, a unique person, a European etc.

pref. not, without.

pref. in, into, on, at, state of.

n. a blood group, excellent grade.

An—*indefinite article*. one, each, any one, per. Used before vowel sounds. As— an orange, an umbrella, an honest boy, an heir etc.

suff. belonging to.

The—When an object is introduced for the first time A/An is used before it, but when something more is added about it , then 'The' is used before it. As—There was a lion in a forest. The lion was hungry. When singular Noun represents the whole class The is used before it. As—The dog is a faithful animal.

Generally The is not used before Proper Noun. But it can be used before some Proper Nouns, the names of religious books, unique things, ordinals, names of rivers, canals, gulf, continent, group of islands, mountain ranges, newspapers, magazines, musical instruments, monuments, historical events. The is also used before Superlative Degree of Adjective.

Above/ Over/On/Upon

Above—in a higher position. As —The bird was flying above the clouds.

	Over—on but not touching. As —The bird was flying over the tree. On—rest on the upper surface of a thing.(touching the thing from upside). As —The bird was sitting on the tree. Upon—on but in the state of movement. As—The dog jumped upon the table.
All together/Altogether.	All together—all in one place, all at once. Altogether—completely, on the whole.
And/ Or	And—is used to add something more while. Or—is used to introduce an alternative. As—He reads Hindi and English. (both). He can study Biology or Mathematics. (one out of the two).
Another Other	*pron & adj.* one more, any other, not the same. *pron & adj.* different, additional, opposite.
Any/Some	Both are used to express quantity or degree. Some is generally used in Affirmative Sentences & Any in Negative & Interrogative Sentences. As—He will give you some tickets. Have you read any book of Kairdas?
Anymore/ Any more	Any more means any longer/ now-a-days. Any more means sth additional or further.
Apart/A part	Apart—*adv.* separated by distance or time. A part—*n.* a piece of sth that forms the whole.
Apostrophe(')	As a Punctuation Mark it indicates the Possessive Case. As—This is Usha's room. As a Figures of Speech Apostrophe is a direct address to the dead, absent or personified object or idea. As—O' Death where is thy sting?
At/In	At is used before the small towns, village etc. while In is used before the big cities or towns. As—He lives at Houdu in Srinagar.
Beautiful/Handsome/ Lovely/Pretty	Beautiful—pleasant to look at (woman). Handsome—pleasant to look at (man). Lovely— beautiful & attractive. Pretty— pleasant to look at (woman).

Because/For/Since/As indicate reason.	Because—denotes the closest casual conjunction (the reason is important). For—denote the weakest conjunction (the reason is given at the end of the sentence). As—reason is already known. Since—the reason is already known. It is formal than As.
Been/Gone	Been—is the p.p. of be, means visited ?& returned. Gone—is the p.p. of go, means visited but not returned yet.
Beside/Besides	Beside is used to show nearness while Besides means in addition to, except. As—Saroj Bala's home is beside a temple. Besides Saroj Bala all the girls were in uniform.
Between/Betwixt/Among	Between—*prep.* in the middle of two. Betwixt—*adv, prep.* between. Among—*prep.* in the middle of more than two.
By/With	By—shows the instrument while. With—shows The agent or doer. As—The snake was killed by Mudit with a stick.
Can/May	Can—as a Modal is used to express power, ability, possibility, permission & nature. May—is used to give & take permission, possibility, wish & prayer.
Cardinal/Ordinal	Cardinal—one, two, six etc. Ordinal—First, second, eighth etc.
Cold/cool/Chilly/ Lukewarm/Tepid	Cold—temperature lower than usual. Cool—cold but pleasant. Chilly—cold but uncomfortable. Lukewarm—slightly warm. Tepid—warm in unpleasant way.
Court of law/ Law court	Court of law—actual room where cases are judged. Law court—it refers to the building.
Each/Every	Both are similar in meaning but Each is used in speaking of two or more things while Every is used

	only in speaking of more than two. Each is used when the number in the group is limited & definite, Every is used when the number is indefinite. As— Each boy in the class is present. Every person in the market was running.
Either/Neither	Either—means one of the two or both. Neither—means not either or none of the two.
Etc/i.e/e.g	Etc—etcetra means and the rest. i.e—id est means it or that is. e.g—exempli gratia means for example.
Every day/Everyday	Every day—each day. Everyday—ordinary.
Farther, Farthest/ Further, Furthest	Farther & farthest—indicate distance. Further & Furthest—indicate degree or extent.
Few/A Few/ The Few	Few—not many, hardly any (negative meaning). As—Few people are satisfied today. A Few—some (positive meaning). As—few students answered the questions. The Few—not many but all there are. As— The few friends he had, proved loyal.
Gerund/Present Participle	Both are formed by adding ing to the first form of the verb but Gerund is a verbal noun while Present Participle is a verbal adjective. Walking is a good exercise. (Gerund) Walking on the road he found a purse. (Present Participle)
Good/Well	Good—is an adjective. It is used when we want to give more information about noun. As—I have a good friend. Well—is an adverb. It is used when we want to give more information about verb. As—Monika speaks well.
Have/Have to	Have—as an auxiliary verb is used to form perfect tense. As—Naseem has gone to her home. Have means possess, to own. As—They have a house. Have to & has to—are used to express obligation in present, had to in past & will have to & shall have to in the future tense. As—Monika has to rise early to attend morning P.T.

Hear/Listen	Hear—to be aware of sounds in the ears. Listen—to pay attention to sb/sth.
Hire/Rent	Hire—is used for hiring for a short period. Rent—is used for hiring for a long period.
How do you do/ How are you	How do you do—It is not a question but a formal way to say Hello. How are you?—It is a question.
In/into	In—*prep, adj.* within an area or space, inside, within a period of time. As —Niharika is in the room *pref.* the opposite of. In is used when any object is inside the certain place. Into—*prep*. the state of going inside from outside. Into is used in the state of going from outside to inside. As— Kailash jumped into the pool.
Its/It's	Its—belonging to it. I have a dog. Its name is Jimmy. It's—it is. It's not your book.
Lay down/ Lie down	Lay down—to do sth following a rule. Lie down—to put body flat.
Little/A little/The little	Little—*adj.* not much, hardly any. A little—some though not much, at least some. The little—not much but all that is there, every thing that is there.
Look/See/Watch	Look—to pay attention, try to see. See—visual impression come to eyes. Watch— look for a time.
Metaphor/Simile	Figures of speech. Simile—is a comparison between two objects of different kinds which have at least one common point. It is introduced by Like, As, So. She is beautiful like rose. Metaphor—is indirect comparison. It is implied Simile. The camel is the ship of the desert.
More/Most	More—used in comparing two objects. Most—used in comparing more than two things.

Most/The most	Most—*adj.* almost all. The most—*adj. & adv.* superlative degree of many.
Much/Many/many a	Much—means a large quantity (with uncountable noun). As—There is much water in the jug. Many—means a great number (with countable noun) As—Many students of JNV qualified IIT exams. Many a—is used with countable noun singular number. As—Many a flower fades unseen.
Never/Seldom	Seldom—means rarely or not often while. Never—means not on any occasion.
Of/Off	Of—Shows possession, it means relating to, from, out of, stating the possessor. Off—Shows separation at a near distance meaning away, out of position, separate.
On/At	On is used before the day & date while. At is used before the time. As—JNV Nainital celebrated its Annual Function On 11th February At 11 A.M.
Ought/Should/Must	*modal verbs.* Ought—to is used to express morality & social binding. Should—is used to express duty, obligation & suggestion. Must—is used to express necessity, compulsion & emphatic advice.
Personal Pronouns	There are three persons of Personal Pronoun. I & We are in First person, You in Second & He, She, They, It in Third persons.
Round/Around	Round—*adj.* circular, whole. *adv.* on all sides, about, here & there. *prep.* in a circle. *n.* a globe, circle. *v.* to turn on. Around—*adv.* on all sides, near.
Shall/Will	*modal verbs.* Shall—is used with first person in simple future & with second & third persons to express threat, promise, determination etc.

	Will—is used to express simple future with second & third person & with first person subject to express promise, willingness, certainty, determination & threat.
Since/For	*prep.* from a time. Since—is used for point of time. For—is used for period of time.
Than/Then	Than—is generally used after the comparative degree of Adjective but comparative degree ending in 'Or' is followed by preposition 'To'. As—Rohit is stronger than Sohail. He is junior to me. Then—means at that time or after that.
The/Thee	The—*definite article.* used to refer to sb/sth that has already been mentioned or is easily understood. *adj.* indicating particular person or thing. Thee—*pron.* *objective & dative case* of *thou.*
Their/There/Theirs	Their—*adj or pron.* of them. There—*adv.* in, to or that place. Theirs—*pron. (used without nouns).*
These/Those	With plural subjects—These for the near objects & Those for the far objects.
This/That	For singular subjects—This for the object near & that for the object far.
Thorough/Through/ Though	Thorough—*adj.* complete, entire. Through—*prep, adv & adj.* from one end or side of another. Though—*adv &conj.* although, despite the fact that.
Thy/They	Thy—*adj. & pron.* pertaining to *thee.* They—*pron. plu.* of he, she, it.
Till/Until	Till—to the time that. Until—till not.
To/Too	To—denotes motion towards anything, from one place to another. As—He went to Tehri Garhwal.

	Too—means also or extreme. Nainital is too cold in winters. Mrigendra is going to his village too.
Who/Whom	Who—is used when it is subject & Whom— is used when it is object.
With/Within	With—shows the company or instrument. As—She went with her father. Within—shows the inside limit of any thing. As—She will return within one month.